THE SUFFERINGS AND THE GLORY
OF THE
LORD'S RIGHTEOUS SERVANT

The Sufferings and the Glory of the Lord's Righteous Servant

By
Robert D. Culver

Wipf and Stock Publishers
150 West Broadway • Eugene OR 97401
2001

THE SUFFERINGS AND THE GLORY OF THE LORD'S RIGHTEOUS SERVANT

By
ROBERT D. CULVER

The Sufferings and the Glory of The Lord's Righteous Servant

By Culver, Robert D.

ISBN: 1-57910-655-2

Reprinted by *Wipf and Stock Publishers*
150 West Broadway • Eugene OR 97401

Previously published by Christian Service Foundation, 1958.

DEDICATION

To my Christian father and mother, Mr. and Mrs. S.C. Culver of Harrah, Washington, I dedicate this book. They brought me up to know and love Jesus Christ my Saviour. Their faith in Him has not dimmed. Their love and loyalty to me have not failed.

ACKNOWLEDGEMENTS

Grateful acknowledgement is hereby given to the following publishers for permission to quote the indicated portions of their publications:

to the SCM Press, Ltd., London, *The Cross in the Old Testament*, H. Wheeler Robinson, 1952, lines from pages 63, 71, 72 and 101;

to Oxford University Press, London, *The Suffering Servant in Deutro-Isaiah*, an Historical and Critical Study, Christopher R. North, 1948, lines from pages 122, 202, 203, and 207;

to the Macmillian Company, New York, *The Messianic Idea in Israel*, from its beginning to the completion of the Mishuah, Joseph Klausner (translated from the third Hebrew edition by W. F. Stinespring), 1955, lines from pages 161-163.

If any copyrighted material is used herein without proper permission and acknowledgement it is entirely unintentional.

FOREWORD

All the Bible, from Genesis to Revelation, was designed by the Holy Spirit to be a revelation of the Redeemer, the Lord Jesus Christ, the Second Person of the Triune God. In biography and in history, in the Mosaic Code and in the ministry of the prophets, in poetry and prose, the Old Testament made preparation for the coming of the Saviour.

Isaiah 53 is the epitome of all prophetical statements about the Coming One, called "the Servant of the Lord." Professor Culver, from his background of devotion to the Lord Jesus and love for the Scriptures, strengthened by his studies in the Hebrew text, gives to us this thoughtful and thought-provoking insight into this key portion of the Scripture.

Comprehension of the prophecy and confidence in the Word of the Living God will be found in these pages, along with a corresponding deepened devotion to the Suffering Servant of the Lord.

— V. Raymond Edman
President, Wheaton College

PREFACE

"The Sufferings and the Glory" is a title borrowed from the Apostle Peter (I Peter 1:11), who used the words to summarize the Old Testament prophecies of the career of Christ. The heart of those prophecies is Isaiah 51:13 - 53:12. Nowhere in all the Bible is the career of our Lord, wherein by a cross He won a crown, more clearly set forth. This book is an exposition of this heartland of Old Testament prophecy.

In substance, these five addresses were first presented, much as they appear here, to a national church conference meeting at Winona Lake, Indiana. Since then this same series has been presented at several Bible conferences. The writer has also presented the material in much more detailed and technical form to his classes in Hebrew Exegesis in two theological seminaries.

Literature continues to appear, in several languages, on this subject each year. In fact several books, monographs, and articles have appeared since the publisher began the work of publication. While I have not attempted to report this literature through this book, revisions have been made to keep the work as up to date as possible.

A chapter treating the identity of the patient sufferer of Isaiah 53 has since been added to make this small book more useful.

The reader will not be amused or even entertained as he reads. There is nothing amusing or entertaining about the cross of Christ. There is, however, much to solemnize, impress, and even thrill one in the cross. Since the death of Christ is never out of sight in Isaiah 52:13 - 53:12 (and I hope never out of sight in these expositions), the reader will of necessity linger long at the cross. May "all the light of sacred story" that gathers at the head of the cross shine on and in.

The citations from the text are from the New Translation which I have prepared and which appears immediately following the table of contents. References to other Scripture portions are from the Authorized Version except in the introductory chapter, where the American Standard Version has been used.

For the benefit of expositors who may wish to see at a glance the general analysis and plan of treatment to follow an outline of the addresses is furnished with the translation.

The writer is conscious of certain oddities of style in the book. These are due in part to the fact that the first five chapters were prepared first for oral delivery. Revision could not fully remove this. The close adherence to the Hebrew text as far as possible and the restrictions of the fifteen verses of the passage account for more. Frequent use of *Jehovah* rather than LORD or the now popular *Yahweh* as the name for Israel's God is due largely to the habit of using the American Standard Version.

CONTENTS

THE TEXT

Isaiah 52:13 - 53:12

I. THE MYSTERY OF THE SERVANT

1. His Exaltation

AUTHORIZED VERSION	NEW TRANSLATION
13 Behold, my servant shall deal wisely; he shall be exalted: and extolled, and be very high.	13 Behold, my servant shall act wisely; he shall be exalted; he shall be lifted up, and shall be very high.

2. Astonishment at His Humiliation

AUTHORIZED VERSION	NEW TRANSLATION
14 As many were astonied at thee; his visage was so marred more than any man, and his form more than the sons of men:	14 Just as many were astonished at thee: (thus disfigured from a man was his appearance and his form from the sons of mankind)

3. Astonishment at His Exaltation

AUTHORIZED VERSION	NEW TRANSLATION
15 So shall he sprinkle many nations; the kings shall shut their mouths at him: for that which had not been told them shall they see; and that which they had not heard shall they consider.	15 So shall he startle many nations; kings shall shut their mouths at him, because that which had not been told them they shall have seen, and that which they had not heard they shall have discovered.

II. THE REJECTION OF THE SERVANT

1. The Rejection of the Message

AUTHORIZED VERSION	NEW TRANSLATION
1 Who hath believed our report? and to whom is the arm of the Lord revealed?	1 Who believed what we heard? And to whom was the arm of Jehovah disclosed?

2. The Rejection of the Person

2 For he shall grow up before him as a tender plant, and as a root out of dry ground: he hath no form nor comeliness; and when we see him, there is no beauty that we should desire him.	2 And he grew up as a suckling-plant before him, and as a root from very dry ground there was no form to him, and no splendor; and we looked at him and there was no good look that we should delight in him.

3. The Nature of the Rejection

3 He is despised and rejected of men; a man of sorrows, and acquainted with grief: and we hid as it were our faces from him; he was despised, and we esteemed him not.	3 He was rejected and forsaken of men, a man of sorrows and acquainted with grief; and as those caused to hide our faces from him so he was despised and we did not esteem him.

III. THE ATONEMENT OF THE SERVANT

1. The Human Occasion

4 Surely he hath borne our griefs, and carried our sorrows: yet we did esteem him stricken, smitten of God, and afflicted.	4. Truly, he himself has borne away our calamity, and as for our sorrows, he carried them. Yet we ourselves did estimate him to be stricken, smitten of God and belabored.

2. The Divine Act

5 But he was wounded for our transgressions, he was	5 And he was pierced for our transgressions; crushed

bruised for our iniquities: the chastisement of our peace was upon him; and with his stripes we are healed.

for our punishments; the chastisement of our peace was upon him, and be his welt healing is for us.

3. The Great Confession

6 All we like sheep have gone astray; we have turned every one to his own way; and the LORD hath laid on him the iniquity of us all.

6 All of us as a flock have gone astray; we have turned each one to his own way, and Jehovah hath caused to strike upon him the punishment due all of us.

IV. THE SUBMISSION OF THE SERVANT

1. In His Suffering

7 He was oppressed, and he was afflicted, yet he opened not his mouth: he is brought as a lamb to the slaughter, and as a sheep before her shearers is dumb, so he openeth not his mouth.

7 He was harassed and belabored, yet did he not open his mouth; and as a sheep to the slaughter he was led, yet as a ewe before her shearers is tongue-tied so did he not open his mouth.

2. In His Death

8 He was taken from prison and from judgment: and who shall declare his generation? for he was cut off out of the land of the living: for the transgression of my people was he stricken.

8 From confinement and from judgment he was snatched away; and among his contemporaries who did consider that he was cut off from the land of living ones on account of the transgression of my people, to whom the stroke was due?

3. In His Burial

9 And he made his grave with the wicked, and with the rich in his death, because he had done no violence, neither was any deceit in his mouth.

9 And there were those who appointed his grave with the wicked ones; yet he was with a rich man in his deaths, because he had done no violence, and there was no fraud in his mouth.

V. THE EXALTATION OF THE SERVANT

1. To Prosperity

10 Yet it pleased the LORD to bruise him; he hath put him to grief: when thou shalt make his soul an offering for sin, he shall see his seed, he shall prolong his days, and the pleasure of the LORD shall prosper in his hand.

10 Yet Jehovah pleased to crush him; he did make him sick. When his soul shall place a trespass offering, he shall see posterity; he shall prolong days; and the plan of Jehovah shall succeed in his hand.

2. To Satisfaction

11 He shall see of the travail of his soul, and shall be satisfied: by his knowledge shall my righteous servant justify many; for he shall bear their iniquities.

11 Because of the travail of his soul he shall see; he shall be satisfied by his knowledge. My righteous servant shall procure righteousness for the many, since he himself bears their punishments.

3. To Compensation

12 Therefore will I divide him a portion with the great, and he shall divide the spoil

12 Therefore I will allot to him a portion among the mighty; and with the power-

with the strong; because he hath poured out his soul unto death: and he was numbered with the transgressors; and he bare the sin of many, and made intercession for the transgressors.

ful he shall divide gain; because he bared his soul to the death, and with transgressors he was numbered; and he himself lifted up the sin of many, and made intercession for the transgressors.

CHAPTER ONE

The MYSTERY of the Servant of the Lord Isaiah 52:13-15

> Behold, my servant shall act wisely; he shall be exalted; he shall be lifted up, and shall be very high.
>
> Just as many were astonished at thee: (thus disfigured from a man was his appearance and his form from the sons of mankind)
>
> So shall he startle many nations; kings shall shut their mouths at him; because that which had not been told them they shall have seen, and that which they had not heard they shall have discovered.

1. The Importance Of The Prophecy

There is much obvious evidence that the passage under consideration (Isaiah 52:13-53:12) is one of the most important in the entire Bible. It appears in the responsive readings, at least in part, of almost every modern hymnal. It is read every Sunday morning in hundreds of Christian worship services all over the world. At the Easter season it has perennially attracted the attention of preachers who sought appropriate texts for their sermons. Missionaries have found it one of the most fruitful of all evangelistic texts. Two centuries ago David Brainerd did some of his most effective missionary preaching to the Indians from texts in this passage.

Perhaps the most distinguished thing about it is the fact that this very portion stands in the background of almost every New Testament treatment of the great events connected with our Lord's passion, death, burial, resurrection, ascension, exaltation, and second coming. The tabernacle and its fixtures, the primeval altars, the high priest's office — these and other things *pictured* these events, but these fifteen verses actually *describe* them in detail.

The Ethiopian eunuch of the eight chapter of Acts memorialized these verses forever in the minds of millions of Bible-reading Christians when after reading that "He was led as a sheep to the slaughter; and like a lamb dumb before his shearer, so opened he not his mouth: In his humiliation his judgment was taken away: and who shall declare his generation? for his life was taken from the earth" he asked, "Of whom speaketh the prophet this? of himself, or of some other man?" Then we read, "Philip opened his mouth, and began at the same scripture, and preached unto him Jesus."

The same passage of Scripture we intend to use for the same important purpose.

2. Its Unique Place In Prophecy

Our passage occupies a unique place in Old Testament prophecy. The prophets, beginning with Samuel, had spoken of an age when God would reign over men through a righteous king. Hopes had been fixed on Saul, then David, and on Solomon. The most pious hearts had been assured that one of these might be that king. But Saul was rejected, David died without "receiving the promise," and Solomon turned out to be a disappointment. Then the kingdom was divided, and even the chosen line of David on the Judean throne at one time became so corrupt that their king Manasseh (II Chronicles 33:9) caused the people to do worse than the abominations of the Canaanites whom the Lord drove out before them. It was at this period, possibly even during wicked Manasseh's reign, that prophecy took a new turn: God's righteous king was to be not only a glorious monarch but a suffering Servant of Jehovah, who would die for the people. There was to be a crown, all right, but before the crown a cross. This was not the usual thing in prophecy. It was a new element. Isaiah 52:13-53:12 is perhaps the first occurrence of it. And down to the resurrection of Christ nobody understood this new approach. Even the prophets themselves, says Peter (I Peter 1:10, 11), "enquired and searched diligently . . . Searching what, or what manner of time the Spirit of Christ which was in them did signify, when it testified beforehand the sufferings of Christ, and the glory which should follow." So, here we have the most important prediction of the "sufferings of Christ" together with some of "the glory which should follow."

Coming now to look at this wonderful anticipation of the career of our Lord, one discerns that it is concerned with one person from beginning to end. That one Jehovah introduces in 52:13 with the words, "Behold my servant." Down to the close of the passage, which concludes "he bare the sin of many, and made intercession for the transgressors," the subject is ever the same.

3. Significance Of Opening Word, "Behold"

It is to be observed that God frequently uses the word "behold" when something important and new is to be revealed. After God made a man who was to live on the earth, he turned to him and remarked, "Behold, I have given you every herb . . . and every tree . . . to you it shall be for food" (Genesis 1:29). And when all the world save eight persons had become corrupt God told the eight, "Behold, I do bring the flood of waters upon the earth, to desstroy all flesh" (Genesis 6:17). To a shocked and surprised Abimelech he said, "Behold, thou art but a dead man." (New and important information it was for Abimelech at least!) So the declaration "Behold, my servant" is intended to introduce something startlingly new and wonderfully important, both to Israel, who first heard it, and to us today.

4. Hebrew Concept Of A "Servant"

A servant in the Hebrew mind (and the Bible is a Hebrew book) was primarily one who did work. The root of the word means that. But because most of the hardest work was often done by slaves, the word came to mean a slave, and this word עבודה is the one so often rendered "bondservant." By extension it came to mean one who, like a slave, had no will of his own, no liberty of his own, save to do the will of his master. How appropriate an anticipation of our Lord, who said, "My meat is to do the will of him that sent me, and to finish his work" (John 4:34)! *Worshippers* of God were His servants, so Nehemiah (1:10) spoke of his brethren in captivity as God's servants. An *ambassador* or *representative* was also thought of as a servant, so Jehovah through Jeremiah spoke of Nebuchadnezzar as "my servant" (Jeremiah 25:9). Any *intimate* of the Lord was thought of as His servant, too — angels (Job 4:18), the *prophets* (Daniel 9:6), *Israel* (Isaiah 41:8, 9), and finally, in the present passage, the Messiah.

"Behold, my servant" — worshipper, ambassador, intimate of Jehovah — who came with no will of His own save to do his Father's will (Luke 2:49, 22:42, John 4:34, 8:29, Hebrews 10:7). Since His Father's will led by Calvary, He drank that cup, saying, "Nevertheless, not my will but thine be done."

This is what the Lord of hosts means when He says, "Behold, my servant."

With these facts in the background, consider this striking portrait of the suffering, dying—living, reigning, man of sorrows, king of glory — the Servant of Jehovah.

First, in 52:13-15 we are reminded of the *mystery* of His career, next in 53:1-3 of His utter *rejection* by His people. Then in 53:4-6 we are told of the *atonement* which He wrought at Calvary and in verses 7-9, of His complete *submission* both to the abuse of man and to the will of the Father. Finally, in verses 10-12 we glimpse something of the transcendent *exaltation* He bought for Himself and for all who by faith make Him the "captain of our salvation."

We consider now the first section, 52:13-15 which presents the mystery of the career of the servant of Jehovah.

The first verse speaks of

THE EXALTATION OF THE SERVANT OF JEHOVAH
(verse 13)

"Behold, my servant shall act wisely; he shall be exalted; he shall be lifted up, and shall be very high."

1. The Success Of The Servant's Career

This presents in outline the stages of Messiah's amazing rise, stage by stage, till finally He reaches what Franz Delitzsch called "an immeasurable height that towers above everything else." In short, verse 13, looking beyond the suffering sees only the glory, the exaltation of the son of God — "far above all principality, and power, and might, and dominion . . . all things under his feet" (Ephesians 1:21, 22). Here are the stages: "he shall rise up; he shall be lifted up, and be very high."

2. The Cause Of His Success

But first the cause of His rise must be seen. It is that He "shall act wisely." Now comes the question: what is this wisdom, this wise activity? A standard dictionary defines wisdom as sound judgment. The so-called wise men of ancient times were what we now call philosophers — men with ability to reflect on the whole of life. We are not, however, left in doubt as to what this wisdom is! It is to follow the direction of the Spirit of God. This is seen in an earlier portion of Isaiah's prophecy (11:2), where he says of this same servant: "And the spirit of the LORD shall rest upon him, the spirit of wisdom and understanding, the spirit of counsel and might, the spirit of knowledge and of the fear of the Lord." Listen to this! Wise activity is that which is directed by the Spirit of Wisdom! It is received in the "fear of the Lord."

Will this bring success? It certainly will. (The word "deal wisely" is translated "have success" in Joshua 1:8.) And, it is said of this same Servant (of Isaiah 42:1-4) — "I have put my spirit upon him." That is the source of His wisdom. But the Lord adds, "He shall not cry, nor lift up, nor cause his voice to be heard in the street." That is, He will not go about paging Himself and bragging about His spirituality. Men can see when one is filled with the Spirit. "A bruised reed shall he not break" —he is easy to get along with. And finally, "He shall not fail or be discouraged till he have set judgment in the earth."

He did succeed. When on His last earthly night he reported in to His Father in the garden prayer He could say "I have finished the work which thou gavest me to do" (John 17:4, A.V.). As He died He cried, "It is finished!" Our redemption was finished. And even though men are now often discouraged (even in the Lord's work), though all the hopeful plans of sinful men must ultimately fail, Jesus is not discouraged, for He "shall not fail." The Christian is in His hands and "he shall not fail." Though the path marked out by the Spirit leads frequently through Gethsemane, the opposition of men, the conniving of the Devil and of his children, even the desertion of our friends — even though there are surely valleys enough and the dark shadow of death, after the cross will come the crown, and beyond the tears there is joy unspeakable.

3. The Stages Of His Rise

The stages of the Servant's rise are three: "He shall rise up; he shall be lifted up, and be very high." The first verb and the second describe the process and the last the result — very high. Some famous expositors see in these three clauses the three well-known stages in our Lord's historical rise: first resurrection, then ascension, and finally, enthronement on high. At least it may be said that there were these three steps in His rise and this may be a veiled reference to them. In the larger aspect, the passage means that before the full results of the work of Christ are accomplished they shall have issued in the exaltation of Christ to such an immeasurable height that words fail to describe it. The utmost force of the Hebrew language is here used to set this forth, and the Greek of the New Testament likewise exhausts its superlatives to explain the utmost height of the Lords exaltation — some of it already past, some yet future. Peter said (Acts 2:33) that He is "by the right hand of God exalted;" Paul, that He "ascended far above all heavens" (Ephesians 4:10) and that God "set him at his own right hand in the heavenly places, far above all principality, and power, and might, and dominion, and every name that is named, not only in this world, but also in that which is to come; and hath put all things under his feet and gave him to be head over all things," and then he adds "unto the church" (Ephesians 2:20-22). (See also Ephesians 1:19-21 and Philippians 2:9.)

However tragic the event appeared to be, the most practical, profitable, and successful event in the history of the world was the death of Christ. It was indeed the event of which it could be said it was "the hour . . . that the Son of man should be glorified" and the hour when the "prince of this world" was "cast out" (John 12:23, 31).

Our text continues with a declaration concerning

AMAZEMENT AT CAREER OF THE SERVANT OF JEHOVAH

(verses 14, 15)

"Just as many were astonished at thee: (thus disfigured from a man was his appearance and his form from the sons of mankind) So shall he startle many nations; kings shall shut their mouths at him; because that which had not been told them they shall have seen, and that which they had not heard they shall have discovered."

There will be a mystery, an incongruity, about the manifestation of the final glory of Christ. How can one so highly exalted be the same meek and lowly carpenter? There was also an incongruity about His past humiliation. How could such perfect humanity be brought as low as He was? These two amazing mysteries are the subject of verses 14 and 15.

1. Two Amazements Observed

The first observation to be made is that *there was an amazement or astonishment described in verse* 14 *that is the measure of another in verse* 15. This is the force of "just as" at the beginning of the former and of "so" at the beginning of the latter. There is a parallel between the two.* This needs emphasis because it is very frequently unobserved. The writer did not see it until he read the passage in Hebrew a few years ago, having missed it in the English for many years. This parallel and comparative relationship is also obscured by the translation of the Hebrew for "startle" in verse 15 by the word "sprin-

*There is another "so" (*Hebrew* כֵּן) in the midst of verse 14, but it is obviously not intended to introduce the apodosis to the first clause of verse 14, It is a part of the protasis.

kle" in our common version. The A. S. V. margin changes it to "startle," which in my opinion is the only possible translation* in such a construction. To be sure, the word is properly rendered "sprinkle" in dozens of other cases. But the situation is like this: in each of the these cases the object of the verb is the *thing sprinkled,* such as water or blood — never the *thing sprinkled upon.* To illustrate, I say: "The priest sprinkled blood on the altar." Never would the construction be dissimilar to that. "The priest

---

*My reasons for the quite dogmatic assertion are as follows:

1) This word is never used with an accusative of the thing which receives the element involved. i.e., the use is, e.g., "He shall sprinkle (נזה .) the blood (the element) upon the altar (the receptacle)." It is never merely, "He shall sprinkle the altar" without naming the element. Leviticus 13:41 is not an exception. Compare Hebrew.

2) The word is always used with the element sprinkled (not the receptacle) in an accusative relation, either supplied or implied.

3) The use of this verb (נזה) in the cognate Arabic shows that it comes from an old Semitic root which may be applied to the leaping up of excess emotion in human beings.

4) The most ancient version (the Septuagint Greek, 3rd century B. C.) so renders it. The Greek word is *thaumasontai* (from *thaumazo*), to look at with wonder and amazement.

5) This inward excitment of all nations at the exaltation of God's Servant accords with the teachings of Scripture (Jeremiah 33:9, Revelation 1:7).

6) This meaning only carries out the parallelism obviously intended to subsist between the reaction to the suffering (v. 14) and the reaction to the glory (v. 15).

7) The idea of the Servant as a priest sprinkling blood is foreign to the context. He is the oblation itself in this case.

8) The explanatory clause following demands this.

So agree many authorities.

sprinkled the altar" could not be said with this Hebrew word. So, the nations in this verse are not the thing sprinkled upon, but rather the object which is agitated like water when it is spurted forth on something else. The nations are "spurted," or more nicely stated, they are "startled." A. B. Davidson, a great Hebraist, said, "It is simple treason against the Hebrew language to render 'sprinkle.' The interpreter who will so translate will 'do anything.' " Those are "fighting words," as we say, for a staid grammarian to use, but they express the general feeling of many competent scholars. The verse teaches that just as Christ in the past shocked mankind in one manner, just so in the future he will shock and startle mankind in another manner.

2. Two Amazements Compared As To Force

The first time Christ came He *astonished* men; but, when He comes the second time He will *utterly shock and stun them.* I must speak again of Hebrew words. The word "astonished" in verse 14, used of the impression on men at the first advent, primarily means to shut up. The idea is extended to refer to the way men shut their mouths in dumb astonishment when some unusual thing happens. There is a form of it translated "desolation" — something horrible and revolting. It is the word used by Daniel and translated "abomination of *desolation*" (Daniel

9:27). There was something very horrible and revolting about the appearance of Christ when He first came that had this effect on men. When He comes again the shock will be worse, for He shall "startle" them. This appearance will stun them. Is this what is in the Spirit's mind in Revelation 1:7, "Behold, he cometh with clouds; and every eye shall see him, and they also which pierced him; and all the kindreds of the earth shall wail because of him"? I do know that the prophecy of Zechariah 12:4 promises that "in that day, saith the LORD, I will smite every horse with astonishment, and his rider with madness: and I will open mine eyes upon the house of Judah, and will smite every horse of the people with blindness."

3. Two Amazements Compared As To Scope

The first time the Servant of Jehovah came the amazement reached *a few individuals* in a small corner of old Syria called Palestine, but when He comes again that Servant will have an aspect which will shock *all nations*. Such is the force of the contrast between "many" and "many nations . . . kings shall shut their mouths." Space fails to tell of the worldwide acclaim and terror when Jesus comes to judge and rule the nations. Many prophecies speak of it.

Modern professional psychology, of which a large percentage is frequently intellectual hypocrisy, has taught us to hide our feelings in the presence of misfortune. A minister is supposed to master a special kind of "bed-side manner" quite like the physician's. That the man of God should express sorrow or grief over sickness, or suggest that a man might not get well is cause for exclamations of alarm, protests, recall, and excommunication. And the worst possible thing a man can do is to be respectfully silent! "Never mind what you say; don't bother whether your words make sense or not; above all say something!" seems to be the philosophy. Our less sophisticated ancestors felt differently about it. When Job's three friends came from a distance and found him desperately ill, they sat down with him upon the ground seven days and seven nights, and none spoke a word to him: "for" the Bible says, "they saw that his grief was very great" (Job 2:13). If a pastor ever behaved in that way towards a sick person of his flock, the members might wish to add execution and dismemberment to excommunication!

But observe! When men saw the suffering and humiliation of Christ they laid their hands upon their mouths in dumb-struck astonishment.

However, blessed thought, when He comes back they will do so again; only the whole earth shall do so, not just the peasants and working people, for "kings shall shut their mouths at him." And well they might, for "He shall have dominion also from sea to sea, and from the river to the ends of the earth . . . Yea, all kings shall fall down before him; all nations shall serve him" (Psalm 72:8, 11).

4. Two Amazements Contrasted As To Nature

Finally, in contrasting these two amazements, we are told that though the first was an amazement of contempt *for* a suffering Servant, the second shall be one of *admiration* for a reigning King.

At the first He was "disfigured from a man . . . and his form from the sons of mankind." The English versions have it that He was "marred *more than* any man." etc. That is grammatically possible but not physically possible, for His body never saw corruption. Two things must be meant. First, His appearance was marred beyond ordinary recognition as anything like the human male in his strength and dignity. Did you ever see the anguish of heart-break on a weeping man's face? If so, then you know what this means. The manly look had vanished. Only in Christ's case the response evoked was not sympathy but contempt. The second thing is that His figure was marred beyond recognition as fully human — "and his figure from the sons of mankind."* Again,

*The Hebrew word for man is איש the male of the human family in his strength and dignity — frequently translated "husband." The word for mankind is אדם the name of the human race, as such. It is also the name of the first man, Adam.

this means not "more than the sons of mankind." It means that He looked like a creature not of our race, so much had sorrow smitten Him.

I do not think we can ever know all about this statement. But I remember what happened in my heart one day when a young man I loved cursed me for trying to help him. I know the pain I felt once when a man whom I thought was a son in the Lord turned his back on me. I remember the distress of a childhood hour when I lost my father's favor for a while. So, I believe I can accept the statement here concerning the injuries His suffering caused and at least in part understand it. The Roman nails didn't hurt too much. Though they pierced His flesh, the thieves felt them also. The thorns pierced His brow, but they may have hurt no more than the tortures of Jeremiah in Zedekiah's dungeon (Jeremiah 39:5, 6). The cross was heavy, but others have carried heavy loads. The curses cut His heart, but others have endured cursing too. No one else, however, ever suffered and died so completely for sins that were entirely not his own as did Jesus; and no man ever died so completely alone in spirit as He. He turned to a Father in whose fellowship He had rested for an eternity, and cried from the depths of His sobbing, heart-broken soul "My God! My God! Why hast thou forsaken me?"

Even the sun ran away and hid his face (cf. Matthew 27:45) when Jesus died. No wonder men clasped hands to their mouths in trembling astonishment! Even the thieves and the callous Roman soldiers were much impressed.

When He comes again* the picture will reverse itself. Men will be astonished rather "because that which had not been told them they shall have seen, and that which they had not heard they shall have discovered." Men who have been taught that Jesus is a man perpetually on a crucifix, or a disappointed Hebrew reformer merely will see something that will shock them more than if the Russian Premier should join the Roman Catholic Church. They shall see the Son of God, this "same Jesus," come "with clouds" of glory. And "every eye shall see him." His glory once was veiled — it is even now veiled from human eyes — but when He comes they shall see it clearly. They shall hear Him, too, for "The sun and the moon shall be darkened and the stars shall withdraw their shining. The LORD also shall roar out of Zion, and utter his voice from Jerusalem: and the heavens and the earth shall shake" (Joel 3:16).

Before leaving these matters, I call attention to an application of this last verse of our text made by

---

*I would not leave the reader with the impression that I regard the explanation of this passage on the basis of the two comings as having been fully perceived before Jesus revealed them (John 14:1-3, Acts 1:11) and the apostles explained them (I and II Thessalonians). Isaiah saw both comings but did not distinguish them (I Peter 1:10, 11).

the Apostle Paul in Romans 15:21. He has just said (verse 20), "Yea so have I strived to preach the gospel, not where Christ was named, lest I should build upon another man's foundation." Then, he adds, quoting our verse from the Greek translation of his day, "But as it is written, 'To whom he was not spoken of, they shall see: and they that have not heard shall understand.' "

One would hesitate to say Paul was interpreting Isaiah 52:15 as directly predicting the preaching of the gospel of Christ in pioneer fields in the age of grace. But this is certain: this expression of Paul's gives us license to believe that when the gospel is preached to men who have not heard, some of them will believe and stand amazed in the presence of the Lord — in the amazement of saving faith toward the wondrous grace of God in saving sinners.

CHAPTER TWO

The REJECTION of the Servant of the Lord Isaiah 53:1-3

> Who believed what we heard? And to whom was the arm of Jehovah disclosed?
>
> And he grew up as a suckling-plant before him, and as a root from very dry ground there was no form to him, and no splendor; and we looked at him and there was no good look that we should delight in him.
>
> He was rejected and forsaken of men, a man of sorrows and acquainted with grief; and as those caused to hide our faces from him so he was despised and we did not esteem him.

In the previous chapter we learned something of the mystery of the Servant of Jehovah. There was mystery in His humiliation and there will be mystery in His coming glory. Above all there was mystery — till the resurrection — concerning the fact that Messiah would be both a patient sufferer and a reigning sovereign.

A glance at the chapter now before us will demonstrate that the verses we have studied (52:13 - 15) are an epitome or preview of the chapter to follow, for the chapter likewise begins with the suffering and ends with the glory.

A PROBLEM: WHO ARE THE CONFESSORS?

A new speaker is introduced in chapter 53 — a group of persons — who speak in the first person. "Who believed what we heard" (verse 1). "We looked at him . . . we should delight in him" (verse 2.) Then mention is made of "our faces" (verse 3), "our calamity . . . our sorrows" (verse 4), and "our transgressions . . . our punishments" (verse 5). So it continues throughout the passage. Who are these ready confessors? Some have said they are the prophets, Isaiah and others, whose message was largely rejected. The Authorized and American Standard Versions seem to support this by their rendering of verse one, "Who hath believed our report?" (A. V.), and "our message?" (A. S. V.). But I think the Hebrew settles the matter, for the word is not "message" or "report" in the sense usually understood. It is a passive participial form of the regular word for hearing a message, and might well be translated, "that which was heard by us." It is the message not from the standpoint of the speaker of the message but from the standpoint of the hearer. The "report" is not "what we said" but rather, "what we heard."

In this light, these words can refer in a primary sense only to Israel. These words fit best in the mouth of Israel of the end-time, who, having then seen both the suffering and the glory, will then understand the mystery and confess Jesus as Lord. They will see then what they had not been told, that He died to save them and has come again both to save and to rule them. This chapter will never have its complete historical fulfillment, in such a case, until Jesus comes back.*

Locale and Circumstances

The prophet Zechariah (12:9 ff.) gives the locale and circumstances. He relates how the Christ-rejection of Israel will at the last bring them to their greatest extremity. In that day not Poland or Russia, not Spain or Germany — but "all nations" shall come against Israel in his land to destroy him. On that occasion, Zechariah relates (Zechariah 12:9, 10), "It shall come to pass in that day, that I will seek to destroy all the nations that come against Jerusalem. And I will pour upon the house of David, and upon

*This was the view of Franz Delitzsch, a very able German Jewish Christian scholar of the 19th century, whose three-volume commentary on Isaiah has gone through many editions in English translation. Delitzsch was a Premillenarian who thus easily accepted this view. Some Postmillennials and Amillinialists have shared an expectation of future conversion of the Jews.

the inhabitants of Jerusalem, the spirit of grace and of supplications: and they shall look upon me whom they have pierced; and they shall mourn for him, as one mourneth for his only son, and shall be in bitterness for him, as one that is in bitterness for his first-born. . ." (See also Revelation 1:7 on this point.)

But having said this,* one must hasten to add that it seems that the spirit of prophecy purposely left the speakers' identity vague. It was in order that anyone could read the verses himself and make himself the confessor — so that I could write my name in there (you could write yours) — and say, "He was wounded for *my* transgressions, was bruised for *my* iniquities."

Nobody who knows in his heart the saving power of Jesus can read this chapter without seeing his own picture in these descriptions of sin, sinners, and of divine forgiveness.

Let us then read and consider these verses in a personal way, realizing that we too were responsible

---

*Some may wonder why, having quoted Zechariah 12:9, 10, I do not continue by quoting also Zechariah 13:6, "And one shall say unto him, What are these wounds in thine hands? Then shall he answer, Those with which I was wounded in the house of my friends." The phraseology seems so applicable to our Lord and so like what one would expect Him to say that there must be some compelling reason for interpreting otherwise. Such there is. The immediately preceding context applies the words to a false prophet, not to the Lord. So agree the majority of critical commentators.

for the rejection and suffering of Jehovah's righteous Servant.

Our attention is now directed to the second section of the oracle, verses one, two, and three of chapter 53, which represents the historical rejection of the Servant of Jehovah.

The first and most obvious fact is

THE REJECTION OF THE MESSAGE CONCERNING HIM
(verse 1)

"Who believed what we heard? And to whom was the arm of Jehovah disclosed?"

1. Rejection of the Message in Words

Historically speaking, Israel rejected the *spoken message* God gave them about their Messiah. The implied answer to the question, "Who believed?" is "Very few or none." What did they hear? They heard the prophets. Jacob said He would be of Judah's tribe (Genesis 49:10); Micah that He would be a Bethlemite (Micah 5:2); Isaiah spoke of His ministry to the poor (Isaiah 9:1 ff. and 61:1). But Herod sought to kill Him, and the leaders of religion took up Herod's cause. They also heard the angels who announced His miraculous birth; they heard the Magi who saw His star; they heard John the Baptist who prepared His way and identified Him when He came. They heard the voice of God from heaven, saying,

"This is my beloved Son, in whom I am well pleased." They heard the seventy; they heard the twelve. Even the demons cried out and bore witness that He was the Son of God. But they did not believe what they heard. Oh, they listened; thousands ate His loaves and fishes, but in the sense of this word "believe," which means full agreement, absolute trust, they did not believe. It is the same word in other constructions and forms often translated "Amen." No one really said Amen to the words of and about Jesus.

2. Rejection of the Message in Deeds

There was another message which Israel rejected besides the spoken one — it was the *message of the works* which Jesus performed. This is brought out in the words, "and to whom was the arm of Jehovah disclosed?"

The "arm" (literally lower or forearm) is a common Old Testament figure of power. An example is Job 22:8. Eliphaz mentions one called the "mighty man." The Oxford Bible margin, true to the Hebrew, renders it, "man of arm." Psalm 79:11 speaks of God as having greatness of "power," but the marginal reading is "arm." Again, Genesis 49:24 in speaking of Joseph's strength strangely refers to it as "the arms of his hands" i.e., the strength of his hands.

In our verse, "was revealed" indicates divine revelation. Now the sense is seen to be "To whom did God make known His power?"

But, someone asks — What power? When? Where? The answer is that the "arm of Jehovah" is clearly those manifestations of God's power in the miracles which Jesus wrought. A common Greek word in the New Testament for the miracles is *dunamis* or power. The people saw the work — the stilling of the waves, the casting out of demons, the raising of the dead, the cleansing of the lepers — but few indeed discerned the God who wrought the works. They said He had cast out devils by the prince of devils. When there was a miracle they could not deny, the leaders shrugged their shoulders. The message of the works of Jesus was seen and understood but not believed, or "discerned" in the spiritual sense of that word.

One may be certain that this interpretation of Isaiah 53:1 is correct, for the New Testament so claims (John 12:37-40): "But though he had done so many miracles before them, yet they believed not on him: That the saying of Esaias the prophet might be fulfilled, which he spake, Lord, who hath believed our report? And to whom hath the arm of the Lord been revealed? Therefore they could not believe, because Esaias said,* He hath blinded their eyes, and hardened their heart; that they should not see with their eyes, nor understand with their heart, and be converted, and I should heal them."

3. The Practical Lesson

The rejection of the message of even our Lord's own words and deeds ought to teach us something important — that saving faith is not brought about by eloquent and convincing speech alone. Neither is it produced by evidence, as such. No event was ever so eloquently described in speech as our Lord's coming. It was likewise well furnished with evidence. He came as the prophets said He would; He presented His credentials and spoke nothing that could not be proved true. But still men did not believe. Why didn't they? They didn't want to. Isaiah says (6:9, 10; cf. John 12:39, 40) that God would not let them. Why didn't God let them? Because they would not let Him! No one can fully explain this — it is one of the mysteries of God past finding out. There are the facts. Convincing argument and evidence can produce conviction but they cannot produce saving faith. That only God can do. It is as Paul says, "No man can

---

*Jesus' use of Isaiah's prophecies incidentally proves that He believed in the unity of authorship of the book called "Isaiah." He quoted Isaiah 53:1 as "the saying of Isaiah the prophet" (John 12:38) and on the same occasion, Isaiah 6:10 (John 12:39-40), as from the same Isaiah. It is quite customary in many scholarly circles to assign the book of Isaiah from chapter 40 onward to a second writer (or a third) living a century and a half later.

say that Jesus is the Lord but by the Holy Ghost" (I Corinthians 12:3). This ought to encourage us to preach courageously as did the rejected prophets of the past, whatever the results; and to pray more earnestly that God himself will give the increase. To Him belongs all the credit in the salvation of even one single soul.

The next step in the story of the Servant's rejection is

THE REJECTION OF THE PERSON OF THE SERVANT (verse 2)

"And he grew up as a suckling-plant before him, and as the root from very dry ground there was no form to him, and no splendor; and we looked at him and there was no good look that we should delight in him."

There is nothing about a message in verse two. It is the person of the Messiah, Himself, who is rejected.

1. Rejected For Rustic Origin

The first reason why sinful men rejected Him was the unpretentious manner of His coming before the nation's attention. Kings are usually born in palaces, reared in rich surroundings, and presented with pomp and splendor. Princes usually grow up before the eyes of all men. But it was not so with this King—

"He grew up as a suckling-plant before him" (that is, before Jehovah).

"Suckling-plant" is the Hebrew *yoneq*, literally a sucker. In the horticultural sense it refers to a layer-sprout, the new plant which springs up when a low branch from a berry bush makes contact with the soil (cf. Job 8:16, 14:7). It is as if, to use an expression we Americans know very well, he was a "hill-billy," a "back-woods" character — just another little bush from the back side of the blackberry patch.

Yes, God knew about Him. God selected the mother. She was a humble woman. God chose the city, a rather remote mountain village in a poor section from the viewpoint of leaders at the center of affairs in Jerusalem. God also chose the home — a carpenter's home — in which He grew up, and God chose the carpenter's vocation He was to follow for a while.

But even though He was God's "beloved Son" and grew up in plain view of Jehovah (and of the hosts of angels) — He was unknown and unsung by men. Only God knew. Even His mother could only "ponder these things in her heart"; she couldn't fully understand.

The result is well-known. Mark relates (Mark 6:2, 3) that "when the sabbath day was come, he began to teach in the synagogue: and many hearing him were astonished, saying, From whence hath this man these things? And what wisdom is this which is given unto him, that even such mighty works are wrought by his hands? Is not this the carpenter, the son of Mary, the brother of James, and Joses, and of Juda, and Simon? And are not his sisters here with us? And they were offended at him."

But, though the hidden life, when like a tender plant or a suckling babe He grew, was an offense to them, it should be a blessing to us, for it sanctified forever the obscure tasks that common people do and the humble places in which common people dwell. He came to do His Father's will. For thirty years His Father's will was a carpenter's shop! Wasted time you say? Not if that was where God wanted Him. Does a home seem an obscure place for your talents, young lady? There is no "career" so blest by the promises of God as that of Christian motherhood. Does a farm seem out of the way, young man? There is no place like a farm to serve God if a farm is God's will for you! And to the preachers let me add: Jesus was prepared to hear one crowd cry, "Hosanna . . . blessed be the king that cometh in the name of the Lord" and another crowd, "Crucify him!" during those quiet years at Nazareth. Moses was great in the kingdom of heaven, and still is, but the will of God for him was forty years on the "back side of the desert."

Let us despise neither the quiet places and the quiet people, nor the quiet years that God may give us.

2. Rejected For Humble Appearance

The second reason sinful men rejected Him was that His appearance when once He made Himself known was not such as would delight unspiritual men. "And as a root from very dry ground there was no beautiful form to him, and no splendor." You will compare these words with the Authorized Version and observe the increased clarity of language. Some have made out from these words that our Lord was an ugly man — ill-formed and mis-shapen. But this statement has no reference to the physical body of Christ.

"A root from very dry ground" probably has reference to the circumstances of the nation when He arose. When this "sprout" or "rod out of the stem of Jesse" — a "shoot" in Israel — grew up, the national soil was never drier. They were in subjection to Rome. Their kingdom had vanished; the throne was extinct; the religious hierarchy was corrupt; and the people were in dispersion. It was indeed "very dry ground." Such a man from such a people was low and despised by the haughty Romans, of course. Since he was very different from what the

Jewish people expected, He was despised by them also.

Three expressions tell us how He looked to Israel: "no beautiful form . . . no splendor . . . no good look." The Authorized has "no form, nor comeliness . . . no beauty." No form" means He had no beautiful form. David is called a "comely person" (I Samuel 16:18) and the word is the same as this. "Comeliness," the word I translate "splendor," is kingly splendor such as is seen in royal courts. In Psalm 21:5, translated "majesty," it is spoken of David's court. "Beauty," which I have rendered "look," is literally just that. There is a play on words. "We looked and there was no good look."

To show how we all attach these special meanings to words when there is nothing intrinsic in the words to give the special meaning, consider how we regard the two words *sight* and *vision.* Ask someone what the difference is between sight and vision, and he will likely say there isn't any difference. We say the the eyes are organs of sight, or organs of vision, and we mean the same. But try this out on your wife when she comes home in a fresh "hair-do" and new dress. Tell her she is a vision to behold and she will purr like a kitten; tell her she is a sight to behold and she may chase you out of the house!

Now in our Lord men saw a "sight," in the most depreciating sense of that word. What did they miss in Him? Not the physical excellence — there is every reason to believe Jesus was a well-formed person. But, there was no *kingly* form, no *regal* majesty, no *royal* appearance. They wanted a *king*, but they got a *carpenter*. They felt like Goliath when the Israelites sent a youth (David) out to fight him. Their egos were insulted.

Let this fact teach us also. There are some great men whose dress is poor, whose diction is provincial. But they call spades spades. They seek no favors and are too honest to "pull strings" or to put better than their usual foot forward. People of God, they are gold — real gold — the thing great saints are made of, the stuff great and good movements run by! There is entirely too much glorying in appearance among us — too much knowing men "after the flesh" (cf. II Corinthians 5:12, 16).

That this resulted in the rejection of our Lord's person is stated by the words, "that we should delight in him." They simply did not want Him! That was the horrible result of judging by appearances; yet men still do it. By the same false principle of judgment some of God's best servants have been judged as of little worth.

We have now approached five of the saddest statements in all the Bible, five statements which set forth the exact details of

THE NATURE OF THE SERVANT'S REJECTION

(verse 3)

"He was rejected and forsaken of men, a man of sorrows and acquainted with grief; and as those caused to hide our faces from him, so he was despised and we did not esteem him."

1. He Was Rejected

"He was rejected," or as the Authorized has it, "He is despised." It was a dreadful thing. The word means to lift the head disdainfully, to treat with contempt, to reject. It is the word used when it is said that Esau "despised" his birthright. It is the most comprehensive of all the terms here, involving that complete act of the whole man when he utterly and completely refuses something.

2. He Was Forsaken

"He was forsaken of men." How true it was. His brethren first forsook Him and then His home town did the same. Nobody welcomed Jesus when early in His ministry He came back home to Nazareth (Luke 4:16-30). Later His many disciples began to go away and He asked even the twelve, "Will ye also go away?" (John 6:66, cf. 7:28). And they did. Finally when with swords and staves they came after Him in the garden, Matthew says, "Then all the disciples left him, and fled" (Matthew

26:56). One may espouse a cause and rejoice to find everybody cheering for him until continued support and friendship mean they may get in trouble along with him and then find himself fighting all alone. That is what happened to Jesus. And even though a handful of His friends gathered to watch Him die, not one of them understood what was happening.

Many have found it not difficult to bear pain and hardness when there were those to cheer. Foreign and home missionary service in lonely spots may not be really very hard if someone publishes your picture and sends a word of encouragement occasionally. But the sorrowful missionary is the one who leaves home and church young, healthy, well-known, and even popular — only to return after years of lonely service to a generation who either never knew him or have forgotten about him.

In the case of our Lord there was not only the loneliness of physical pain (the thieves at least shared that), but there was the loneliness of complete misunderstanding. There is no evidence that even His mother, or John, or the friendly women at the cross understood just why He "laid down his life." In fact, He was not only forsaken of men; even God turned His face away. In such loneliness, in that terrible hour, the Saviour of the world bowed His noble head and died. The following poem by Ben H. Price, especially the sixth line, expresses what I mean.

It was alone the Saviour prayed In dark Gethsemane;
Alone He drained the bitter cup And suffered there for me.
It was alone the Saviour stood In Pilate's judgment hall;
Alone the crown of thorns He wore, Forsaken thus by all.
Alone upon the cross He hung That others He might save;
Forsaken then by God and man, Alone, His life He gave.

Alone, alone, He bore it all alone;
He gave Himself to save His own,
He suffered, bled and died, alone, alone.

3. He Was An Offence

He was an offence. I read, "We hid as it were our faces from him." What did it mean? There are several things that cause people to hide their faces — shame or shock or contempt will do it. The last, contempt, is the case here. He was not truly contemptible. His presence was always a blessing: He made the best wine for a wedding; He produced food for the hungry; He healed the sick; He opened the eyes of blind men and cleansed lepers; He tamed a wild man; He even broke up a funeral and restored the corpse of a man alive to his household. But still they turned their faces in contempt. When He healed a man they complained because it was on the Sabbath. When He claimed to be the Son of God, they called it blasphemy. They called "evil good and good evil . . . put light for darkness and darkness for light." If Jesus had lived in our generation, the meteorologists would have jailed Him for breaking up a storm they had predicted; the undertakers would have complained that His actions implied they had buried Lazarus alive. The Democrats would have damned Him for fellowship with a (Re)publican and the Republicans for featherbedding the carpenters' union! The physicians would have complained about His robbing them of their business and the lawyers for encouraging Christians to disavow their services. Nothing He might do could possibly be "right" in the eyes of His countrymen.

It's a strange world. The wheels are out of gear. If it were not, it would never have hid its face from such a Saviour.

4. He Was "Contemptible"

"He was despised." It is the same Hebrew word as the first of this series — the same as translated "rejected" earlier in the verse. I want to add here that all the contempt and hate possible is poured into this word. The most hated, despised, and villainous man in Hebrew history is probably Antiochus Epiphanes, who in about 165 B.C. robbed and then profaned the Jewish temple by offering heathen sacrifices on the brazen altar. To the Jewish mind there could be nothing worse. Yet Daniel in describing Him uses the same word — a "contemptible person" (Daniel 11:21). Jesus, in the minds of these men, was in the same class with the reprobate who desecrated the holy altar with the carcass of a sow!

5. He Was Unesteemed

Finally, He was unesteemed; "And we did not esteem him." The word is elsewhere rendered "impute." Of Abram it is said that God "imputed to him righteousness." But to Jesus men did not impute anything good. He was just "no good," worthless, unfit to be their Messiah.

We are told what it did to our Lord Jesus. Human beings react to praise or blame, to love or hate, to esteem or contempt, and Jesus was a human being. It made him "a man of sorrows." Of Israel in Egyptian bondage, God said, "I know their *sorrows*" (Exodus 3:7); Job spoke of the "*pain*" (Job 3:19); and the Lamentations of Jeremiah speak of the "*grief*" that poor man suffered — in each case the Hebrew word is the same. Jesus knew sorrows, pain, and grief. None of these other men suffered the sorrow Jesus did. And because of it He became "acquainted with grief." He knew it in others for He lived among the poor, the weak, the sick, the suffering; widows and orphans were a primary concern. He knew it in

Himself. Above all, His conflict with sin brought grief upon Him, and when He took our sins upon Him, then sin brought a grief that could only break His heart and kill Him. We can almost hear Him say

> I am the man that hath seen affliction by the rod of his wrath.
> He hath led me, and brought me into darkness, but not into light.
> He hath turned aside my ways, and pulled me in pieces: he hath made me desolate,
> He hath bent his bow, and set me as a mark for the arrow.
> I was a derision to all my people; and their song all the day.
> He hath filled me with bitterness, he hath made me drunken with wormwood.
> He hath also broken my teeth with gravel stones, he hath covered me with ashes,
> And thou hast removed my soul far off from peace: I forgat prosperity.
> And I said, My strength and my hope is perished from the LORD:
> Remembering mine affliction and my misery, the wormwood and the gall.
> My soul hath them still in remembrance, and is humbled within me.
>
> (from Lamentations 3:1 - 20)

This experience of our Lord was something ultimate. It had to be if He was to bear the sin of the world. As such it is occasion both for our joy and sorrow: joy that we have a complete and sure redemption, joy that our Saviour knows how to help us in suffering; sorrow that it was our sin as well as theirs that nailed Him there. This mingled joy and sadness has probably never been better expressed than in the poem "Man of Sorrows."

"Man of sorrows," what a name
For the Son of God who came,
Ruined sinners to reclaim!
Hallelujah! What a Savior!

Bearing shame and scoffing rude,
In my place condemned He stood;
Sealed my pardon with His blood;
Hallelujah! What a Savior!

Guilty, vile and helpless, we;
Spotless Lamb of God was He;
"Full atonement;" can it be?
Hallelujah! What a Savior!

Lifted up was he to die,
'It is finished," was His cry;
Now in heav'n exalted high;
Hallelujah! What a Savior!

When He comes, our glorious King,
All His ransomed home to bring,
Then anew this song we'll sing:
Hallelujah! What a Savior!

CHAPTER THREE

The ATONEMENT of the Servant of the Lord

Isaiah 53:4-6

> Truly, he himself has borne away our calamity, and as for our sorrows, he carried them. Yet we ourselves did estimate him to be stricken, smitten of God and belabored.
>
> And he was pierced for our transgressions; crushed for our punishments; the chastisement of our peace was upon him, and by his welt healing is for us.
>
> All of us as a flock have gone astray; we have turned each one to his own way, and Jehovah hath caused to strike upon him the punishment due all of us.

One day in August, many years ago — 1930 to be exact — one of my boyhood dreams came true. Every morning of my life I had stepped out of the house and looked westward at the majestic eastern slope of the Cascade Mountains of central Washington. The snowy white of winter, the green of spring, the brown overhung by evergreen and topped by the towering peaks of 12,000-foot Mount Adams and

14,408-foot Mount Ranier had always intrigued and invited me. Father, Grandfather, and Great-grandfather had ridden those ridges and canyons for three generations — hunting, fishing, vacationing, herding sheep and punching cattle — almost back to the close of the Indian wars. Oh, I had been along the main roads on many camping and fishing trips, but never "away back" in the shadows of the crags and beside the glaciers and the Goat Peaks.

Then, on this day, my father took us for a week's horse-back trip. There were always at least two saddle-horses at our place and a farm horse that would do for a pack-horse. Our Indian neighbor furnished another buckskin cayuse and off we went — Papa, my 11-year-old sister, Julia; seven-year-old brother, Gail; and 14-year-old I. I started ahead of the rest with the string of horses at 4:00 o'clock in the morning. By eleven o'clock I had ridden 27 miles to where the road ended and there I waited till the others came in the car. After a brief lunch Mama and the baby sisters went home in the car and we started the climb. Even 25 years have not dimmed my indescribable exhilaration and ecstasy as we mounted those dreamy pine-covered ridges. The pine soon gave way to fir and spruce and aspen at higher levels. Then, up ahead my father rode "Ole Buck" out on a slight outcropping of rock and drew up to a stop. I saw him look into a circle of trees 10 yards to his right and below, then dismount, and with grave face go to the spot toward which he was looking. When he arrived he turned to me and said, "Come here, Bob!" I came and looked, and in that spot saw the skulls of about 20 horses laid nose to nose in a five-foot circle. Many winters before, my father said, an early snow had trapped them all there and they had died of starvation.

Then I learned that beautiful and majestic as the mountains are, they are deadly too. Human bones are hid at the foot of many a cliff and glacier. Death and misery are there. It almost spoiled my trip for the rest of the day thinking about it.

To apply the picture, we are in a wonderful country here in this chapter. All the glory of the wondrous cross of Jesus shines through, and up ahead towers the coming city of God. But there is sorrow here; there's tragedy; there's the blackest thing in all the universe — sin, together with the starkest tragedy the world has ever seen, the death of the Lord of life.

Neither the word *sin* nor any of its synonyms has been mentioned in the two sections treated in our first two chapters, but now sin studs the landscape in every direction in all its manifold aspects. It is in verse 12, "he bare the sin of many." This word describes sin in its negative aspect. A form of it is translated "miss" in Judges 20:16. It means to come short of the glory of God. Sin is in verse eight: "for the transgression of my people was he stricken." Transgression is sin in its positive aspect. It is open rebellion and revolution against law and authority, and is so translated many times (cf. II Kings 3:5, 7; 8:20). But the most dreadful of all its aspects is in the section before the reader now. "He was bruised for our iniquities"* (verse 5). I have rendered it "punishments." It has special reference to the wholeness of sin, resulting in guilt and punishment. It is the word Cain used when he said (Genesis 4:13), "My punishment is greater than I can bear."

Rebellion, falling short, punishment — sin in both positive and negative aspects together with its awful result is here.

It is with God's means of forgiving this sin that we are now concerned. There is a sense in which it may be said that sin is never forgiven, though sinners are. Sin is always punished — if not in the sinner then in his substitute. Now our Lord reveals to us in the three verses before us (Isaiah 53:4-6) how our sin came to be punished and we came to be forgiven. It is the story of "The Atonement of the Servant of Jehovah." He reveals the human occasion, verse

---

*Precisely how God has treated each of these aspects of sin is set forth in Psalm 32:1, 2. I suggest the following translation: "Oh, the blessedness of him whose *rebellion* is lifted up, whose *failure* is covered over. Oh, the blessedness of the man unto whom Jehovah imputes not *punishment*." Every word speaks of our Lord's atoning death.

four; the divine act, verse five; and the great confession concerning it, verse 6.

Consider first,

HUMAN OCCASION FOR ATONEMENT OF THE SERVANT
(verse 4)

"Truly, he himself has borne away our calamity, and as for our sorrow, he carried them. Yet we ourselves did estimate him to be stricken, smitten of God and belabored."

The very first word introduces the section as an explanation of what has gone before. That is the significance of the word "surely" or "truly."* Why was He rejected? The reasons are these:

1. Occasion In The Punishment Due Men

First, there were the punishments due men which He bore. They are called "calamity" and "sorrow."

"He himself has borne away our calamity." The word "calamity" is punishment objectively considered — a dreadful thing, unpleasant experience both physical and mental, sickness and insanity. All the dis-

---

*This word, אכן is of strong asseverative force, emphasizing sharp contrast with what has preceded and indicating that an explanation is about to follow (cf. same in Genesis 28:16; I Samuel 15:32). The movement of thought may be paraphrased: Converted Israel says (vv. 1-3), When Christ came the first time it was to suffer and die in rejection, *but the explanation is* (אכן) as follows (vv. 4-6), etc.

tress to body, soul, and spirit that hell will be is wrapped up in this word, as well as all the present effects of sin. We do not bear it forever because He bore it. The word "borne" calls for attention. It is the word Cain used when he said, "My punishment is greater than I can bear" (Genesis 4:13). It is used in the story of the scape goat where it is said the goat "bore" the sins of Israel (Leviticus 16:22) into the desert. It is the word "forgiven" in Psalm 32:1, "Blessed is he whose transgression is forgiven." Our punishment could not be remitted; it had to be borne. We could not bear it, so Jesus did.

"And as for our sorrows, he carried them."* Sorrow is the subjective emotional side of calamity, calamity (punishment) the dread result of sin. Jesus truly suffered. They were real sorrows. Our Lord's experience was something more than an official and judicial thing. It was real and personal, too. If God in

---

*The meaning of these two parallel clauses ("he himself has borne away our calamity, and as for our sorrows, he carried them") is that He not only outwardly and objectively bore objective sentences and punishments, but also inwardly and subjectively bore the subjective results in grief and torment which naturally result.

The citation of this portion in Matthew 8:17, wherein it is used as a prediction of the healing ministry of our Lord, is to be regarded as fully proper but not an exhaustive explanation of its meaning. Matthew frequently quotes the Old Testament in this way (cf. 2:15, 23). Indeed, inasmuch as His healing ministry was a partial remission of the full effects of sin it was a pledge of the full remission at Calvary later. Healing for the body was provided in the atonement, for physical death is one of the results of sin in Adam which must be remitted for full redemption. However,

heaven held it as lightly as we often quote John 3:16, it would not amount to much. Emphasize the right part too —he took *our* sorrows, and *our* calamity. What would have been personally mine He made personally His.

Oh what a vale of tears we live in! Hundreds of people die every hour. The doors of our hospitals are open every minute. The graves fill by the hour many times over. I've seen the tortured frames of those injured in automobile accidents. I've watched them fight to live and finally die. I've held their hands and the hands of their parents as the shadows drew nigh. My shoulder has been the pillow for the tears of wicked girls and boys. I've seen the stark and awful heart-break of a breaking home. I've seen a little of the sadness of good-by. One of these days you and I shall enter a door beyond which "God will wipe away all tears from their eyes, and there shall be no more death, neither sorrow, nor crying, neither shall there be any more pain." Heaven will be free of tears!

---

full benefit will be received at the resurrection and glorification of the saints — and not until then. Frequently, when it suits His purpose, God gives us some of those benefits in healing now. There is absolutely no sound Scriptural basis for the belief that healing of the body is the will of God for all saints, and that sickness is evidence of either lack of faith or special personal sin. The procedure for asking God for healing of the bodies of believers is given in James 5:13-16, but it is significant that in the same passage the benefit and grace of God in permitting sickness to be patiently endured is pointed out.

And why? Because Jesus wrung them out at Calvary. No wonder Peter spoke of the "precious blood."

So much for one side of the human occasion of the atonement.

2. Occasion In Misunderstanding Of His Sinless Character

The other side is the very human misunderstanding of the character of Jesus as the sinless "holy one of God." They simply didn't see that He had no sins of His own for which to die. The verse says, "Yet we ourselves did esteem* him to be stricken, smitten of God and belabored." They made an estimate of Jesus, all right, but they decided that God was punishing Him for His own sins. This statement, so often used as the right interpretation of Jesus' death, is really the wrong one. "Stricken" is the customary word for a divine judgment of some kind. When God caused King Uzziah to become a leper** it is said "the Lord

---

*The word is *chashabh,* the same translated "imputed" in Genesis 15:6. This is a good illustration of what imputation is.

**In the Babylonian Talmud 98b, we read: "The Messiah — what is his name? ... The Rabbis say, The leprous one of the house of Rabbi is His name, as it is said surely He hath borne our griefs... yet we did esteem Him stricken, smitten of God and afflicted."

The basis of this is in the word "stricken," (נגוע), the root of which is several times in the Old Testament used of being stricken with leprosy.

had smitten him." The other words in the clause have the same general meaning. So, here is the reason they committed Him unto death — they thought that for His own sins He ought to be "stricken, smitten of God, and belabored."

The Gospel records bear this out. Pilate could find no fault in Him, but the Jews could. They crucified Him in the name of God for two capital offences — sabbath breaking and blasphemy. John 5:18 reports, "Therefore the Jews sought the more to kill him, because he not only had broken the sabbath, but said also that God was his Father, making himself equal with God."

What then were the human occasions of the atonement of Christ? They were, first, the guilt of mankind, which made substitutionary atonement the only possible method of salvation; and second, the misunderstanding of sinful men concerning Christ's holy character, which resulted in their nailing Him to a cross, where He died in their stead.

"Why hast thou forsaken me?" On two counts we are the answer to the cry — the first our guilt, the second man's blind misunderstanding of the Saviour's character and mission.

Do not blame the Jews for the crime any more than ourselves. It was our sin that nailed Him to the tree. Each lie of ours is a cry to "crucify him"; each hateful word a nail in His hand; each selfish thought a thorn in His brow; each blaspheming oath a spike through His feet; each unbelieving day a thrust through His side.

Now, let us look at

DIVINE ACT IN THE ATONEMENT OF THE SERVANT

(verse 5)

"And he was pierced for our transgressions; crushed for our punishments;* the chastisement of our peace was upon him, and by his welt healing is for us."

Who Killed Jesus?

It is now not uncommon for some more liberal-minded Jewish rabbis to admit that the Jews may have been wickedly responsible for Jesus' death and to say they are now sorry. Some of them are even rather proud to own Him as another good but misunderstood Jewish prophet. In other generations the Jews have vehemently denied any charge of guilt for crucifying the Saviour, and attempts are still made to exonerate themselves.**

---

*Some Hebraists may recoil from "punishment" as translation of עון Yet it does have precedent in the standard versions and lays emphasis on the wholeness of the wrong in sin, including the penalty for it. The author would welcome the suggestion of a more comprehensive and useful word.

**An article by Samuel Rosenblatt ("The Crucifixion of Jesus from the Standpoint of Pharisaic Law," *Journal of Biblical Literature*, Dec. 1956) attempts to prove that the Pharisees, at least, had nothing

Be that as it may, there was a greater act than man's, a greater power than man's involved when Jesus died. Men killed Him, but God planned it so. Both the wickedness of man and the plan of God were at work. Therefore, Acts 2:23, addressed by Peter to the Jews who killed Him, says, "Him, being delivered by the determinate counsel and foreknowledge of God, ye have taken, and by wicked hands have crucified and slain." There is something about this mystery that must be accepted by faith, something that mere human understanding cannot sound.

In this verse, the divine act whereby God actually inflicted His wrath for sin upon Christ is indicated by the passive voice of all the verbs — "was pierced . . . was crushed." God is emphatically the actor.

1. The Nature Of The Punishment He Bore

Four expressions tell us what God did to Jesus when He punished Him for our sin.

He Was Pierced.

The first is "pierced" — "He was pierced for our transgressions." It seems to me it can refer to nothing directly except the driving of the nails into

---

to do with it, that the Romans apparently were responsible, and that the New Testament record has an anti-Jewish cast in regard to the crucifixion of Jesus. This cast, it is contended, was imported to the story after Christianity became predominantly Gentile.

His hands and feet and the thrust of the spear into His side.

He Was Crushed

The second is "crushed" — meaning to be utterly and fully broken and bruised. He was crushed, *physically*. The treatment He received beginning with the slap on the face and concluding with the thrust of the spear was crushing though only in a limited degree. More than that He was crushed *emotionally*. He loved these folk who were killing Him. He had wept over their city and had spent the last week of His life preaching to them. This was worse than being "voted out." The rejection of love and care is the supreme indignity.

He Took Chastisement

The third is "reproof" or "chastisement." It is penal punishment in this case (not corrective like our chastisement as Christians) such as dealt to law-break ers. In Ohio it would be the gallows, in Indiana the electric chair, in Utah the gas chamber, in France the guillotine, in the army the firing squad, but in the Roman Empire it was what has been called the most cruel kind of public execution ever devised — crucifixion.

He Received Welts

The fourth is "welt" or "stripe." The word refers to the mark left by a club or whip. It reminds us that "Pilate therefore took Jesus and scourged him" and that the soldiers "took the reed and smote him on the head."

But, specific as all these terms seem to be, detailed as the fulfillment seems to have been, it appears to me that all these things only symbolize the worst part of the suffering, something no Old Testament prophet could see. I refer to the severance of the fellowship that took place when the Father turned away and the Son cried out in the bitterness of abandonment, "My God! My God! Why hast thou forsaken me?" That pierced Him more deeply than the spikes and spear did. That crushed Him more than the weight of the cross He carried up the hill. That was sterner reproof than anything Roman or Jew had devised for criminals; and *that made a welt in His heart where the whip couldn't reach.*

2. The Vicarious Value Of His Experience

The vicarious, substitutionary value of the suffering and death of Jesus is indicated by two expressions: "for our transgressions . . . for our punishments."

In consideration of this fact in the opinions of men we meet the problem of what has come to be called "double talk." A noted preacher is perfectly willing to say he believes that all suffering is vicarious and add in the same breath that the doctrine of the blood atonement is "a perversion of the Christian Gospel." What does he mean? Probably merely that those who cause suffering eventually suffer more than those who endure their wrongdoings, or that the sight of suffering serves to chasten men. This man surely means to say that our salvation has no relation to what Christ did *for* us. As we intend it to be understood, vicarious means substitionary. When I say the death of Christ was vicarious, I mean that He died *in my place.*

"He was pierced for our transgressions; crushed for our guilt." One of the most discerning and well-informed students of the Hebrew Old Testament, if not most original, was Dr. Albert Barnes. He said concerning these words that if it is possible for human speech to describe substitutionary atonement, these words to do so. Franz Delitzch — than whom few more learned and discerning Old Testament scholars ever lived — said that such is the only possible construction to be placed on these words. Our transgressions and sins actually caused His death. One may deny substitutionary atonement, but he cannot do it and believe the Bible!

Bearing shame and scoffing rude,
In my place condemned He stood;
Sealed my pardon with His blood;
Hallelujah; What a Savior!

Verse four tells us that Israel once thought God was punishing Jesus at Calvary for His own sins. In verse five a convicted and repentant Israel, who have learned that the wounds in His hands were made there for their sins, confess that God was punishing Him in their stead. The first is the wrong view: the second is the right.

3. The Atoning Effects Of His Experience

The atoning value of that death is set forth in two expressions which present the results of His work: "Our peace . . . healing is for us."

Peace

"Peace" (שלום) is one of the most important words in the Old Testament. We think of peace as one of two things: cessation of activity (that is, rest) or as the termination of hostility — the end of warfare. The Hebrew word includes both and more besides. This will appear as one considers some of the translations of שלום *in* the Authorized Version: "It is *well*" (Genesis 29:6), "in *good health*" (Genesis 43:28), "Is Absalom *safe?*" (I Samuel 18:29), "I saw the *prosperity* of the wicked" (Psalm 73:3), "*wholly* carried away" (Jeremiah 13:19). An amazing use is in II Samuel 11:7 where David inquires of Uriah concerning the war Joab is waging. Hold in mind that Joab and the people were waging bitter warfare, and note the literal rendering: "David demanded of him concerning the peace of Joab, and concerning the peace of the people, and concerning the peace of the war." Our Authorized translation makes better sense to us, but the literal rendering helps in seeing the breadth and depth and height of this word "peace" — health, wholeness, safety, prosperity, soundness. It describes more fully than any other single word just what Christ procured for us at Calvary — deliverance "from wrath" and procurement of "all things that pertain to life and godliness." It was typified in the Peace-offering.*

HEALING

Along with this goes "healing" — "by his welt healing is for us." This is both judicially true and practically true — official in the reckoning of God and experiential in the life of the believer. Every spiritual disease was healed for us in Christ and the physical ones, too. Some are now in effect, some are going into effect, some will not reach actuality till Jesus comes again, but even now judicially it is all "ours." We own it all though we do not possess it

---

*The שלם or peace-offering in a remarkable way presented the benefits of salvation for all concerned. With this offering a joyful feast was always connectted. The Lord had His portion, the inner parts of the slain animal, which were burned for Him on the brazen altar; the priests ate a thigh and a shoulder; the offerer and his friends could eat the remainder in the tabernacle precincts. Thus both God and His people could be seen to receive benefit. For the people it meant joy, health, happiness, peace, prosperity. In the New Testament we are told that Christ "is our peace."

all. That is the primary meaning of "healing is for us." But in another way "his welt" brings healing to us. I mean that the welts raised on our Redeemer are each a lesson to cause us to turn from our sins. No one who realizes that each one of his sins adds another burden to the weight of Calvary is likely to continue on a wilful, sinful way. That is why it is good to contemplate the cross long and often, and why I say the healing has a practical realization now in holiness as well as primarily a judicial realization in righteousness.

Having now seen the human causes and the divine act, there next comes

CONFESSION CONCERNING ATONEMENT OF SERVANT (verse 6)

Israel now confesses three things: 1) that man is a sinner by nature, collectively in Adam ("All of us as a flock have gone astray"); 2) that man is a sinner by choice individually ("we have turned each one to his own way"); and 3) that the punishment for both, which is man's due, was all laid on Christ ("And Jehovah hath caused to strike upon him the punishment due all of us").

1. Man Is Sinful By Nature — As A Race

Mankind are collectively sinners by nature; that is, born with guilt for Adamic sin, with an inborn inclination to sin. Man is not neutral with equal propensities for either good or for evil. His propensities, however good in a relative sense, all fall short of the true good, which is the glory of God who made him.

Such is the teaching of this first clause, "All of us as a flock have gone astray." "All of us" means all the confessors. Of course, primarily these are the restored Israel, but we have already shown how that all redeemed men do join the confession. There are no exceptions. Though some men may not be so wicked as others, all men do have an inherited sinful nature. The words "as sheep" are, as I have translated, properly, "as a flock." Sheep do not behave as individuals in moving from one area to another. An anyone knows who has ever handled sheep, they follow a leader and move as a flock. Thus all of us did in Adam (whose name in Hebrew, by the way, means mankind). The words "gone astray" are also so translated in Psalm 58:3, which significantly says, "The wicked are estranged from the womb: they go astray as soon as they be born." Again, the Psalmist says, (119:176) "I have gone astray like a lost sheep." Now it is obvious in all these cases that to "go astray" involved no act of reflective thought or movement of the will. Adamic nature and guilt are ours without any acts of our own. We got them at our conception before we could think, as David says,

"In sin did my mother conceive me" (Psalm 51:5). He meant not that his mother was an immoral woman, nor that the act of parents which produces conception is wrong, but that from conception onward he, David, had a sinful nature.

May I emphasize that this is the New Testament doctrine, and that the New Testament emphatically declares that guilt and punishment are deserved, even for this in-born sin. I cite Romans 5:12, "Wherefore, as by one man sin entered into the world, and death by sin; and so death passed upon all men, (as a punishment for sin, obviously) for that all have sinned." This is why the heathen are lost, and why except for the atonement of Christ, which goes as far as depravity, every infant who dies would go to hell. Hard doctrine, you say? Yes, many hard things are also true.

2. Man Is Sinful By Choice — As A Person

Furthermore, men are individually sinners by choice — "We have turned each one to his own way." Every word in this clause speaks of personal, wilful, deliberate action. Our sinful nature expresses itself in decisions of the whole man (i.e. the will) which agree with it. This is what the Psalmist is speaking of (Psalm 14:2, 3): "The LORD looked down from heaven upon the children of men, to see if there were any that did understand, and seek God. They are all gone aside, they are all together become filthy:

there is none that doeth good, no, not one." To be convinced that the New Testament teaches this same doctrine, one need only turn to the third chapter of Romans where the condemnation of the whole race is pronounced for inbred sin — and these very same words from this very same Psalm are quoted as proof-texts.

3. Jesus Bore The Results of Both Racial And Personal Sin.

Finally, to show that Jesus took the guilt and punishment for all mankind's sin and sins, whether racial or personal, whether inbred or wilful, the text declares as our confession, "And Jehovah hath caused to strike on him the punishment due all of us."

Almost the whole plan of salvation is in this brief statement. Jehovah God Himself is the actor. Salvation is all of God. In Him is justification, sanctification, and glorification. This is emphasized in II Corinthians 5:19 — "God was in Christ, reconciling the world unto himself." Man had nothing to do with it. God was the agent. Furthermore, salvation or forgiveness of sins is with respect to punishment — and that not by simple failure on God's part to inflict punishment. God always punishes sin. The word "iniquities" of our common version really includes everything about sin — disposition, act, sins of omission and commission, together with the guilt and punishment of the same. Punishment is only the result and final consummation. Hence, it has been translated in the Authorized Version "fault," "iniquity," "mischief," "punishment of iniquity." All of this, reads the Authorized Version, the LORD "laid on him." How tame a rendering! Let us read a few passages where the word translated "laid" is used. "And the children of Dan said, . . . Let not thy voice be heard among us, lest angry fellows *run upon* thee, and thou lose thy life" (Judges 18:25). "And king Solomon sent by the hand of Benaiah the son of Jehoiada; and he *fell upon* him that he died" (I Kings 2:25). "So Benaiah the son of Jehoiada went up, and *fell upon* and slew him" (I Kings 2:34). Thus is the death of Joab described. If you want to know what it means to have "iniquity" laid upon one, ask Joab. It meant death to him, capital punishment for sin. So it was with Jesus. All the hell that the Lake of Fire will be for lost men, Jesus took in that dreadful afternoon on Calvary.

Finally, observe that the verse closes as it began — "All of us ... all of us." Praise God, though sin went deep and far, redemption goes farther still. "Where sin abounded, grace did much more abound" (Romans 5:20). "For if by one man's offence death reigned by one; much more they which receive abundance of grace and the gift of righteousness shall reign in life by one, Jesus Christ. Therefore as by the offence of one judgment came upon all men to condemnation; even so by the righteousness of one the free gift came upon all men unto justification of life" (Romans 5:17, 18).

Yet one more thought. Many arguments have been angrily fought out and much blood has been shed over the question of who killed Jesus. The truth is that in one sense the Romans killed Him; a Roman soldier drove the nails into His hands and another thrust the spear into His dead body. In another sense the Jews killed Him, for it was a Jewish mob which yelled, "Crucify him!" In still another sense we all killed Him, for it was in our place and for our sins that He died. But in the most real and important sense — one almost shudders to say it, though it is true — God killed Him, "ran upon him that he died," for — and I return to our last verse — "Jehovah caused to strike on him the punishment due all of us."

The heart of the saint can only cry out, as he contemplates and believes all this:

Praise ye the Lord

> Praise God in his sanctuary:
> praise him in the firmament of his power.
>
> Praise him for his might acts:
> praise him according to his excellent greatness.
>
> Praise him with the sound of the trumpet:
> praise him with the psaltery and harp.

Praise him with the timbrel and dance:
praise him with stringed instruments and organs.

Praise him upon the loud cymbals:
praise him upon the high sounding cymbals.

Let everything that that breath praise the LORD.
Praise ye the LORD.

CHAPTER FOUR

The SUBMISSION of the Servant of the Lord Isaiah 53:7-9

> He was harassed and belabored, yet did he not open his mouth; and as a sheep to the slaughter he was led, yet as a ewe before her shearers is tongue-tied so did he not open his mouth.
>
> From confinement and from judgment he was snatched away; and among his contemporaries who did consider that he was cut off from the land of living ones; on account of the transgressions of my people the stroke was his?
>
> And there were those who appointed his grave with the wicked ones; yet he was with a rich man in his deaths, because he had done no violence, and there was no fraud in his mouth.

In considering the first verse of this passage (52:13) it was pointed out that our Lord is Jehovah's Servant. It is appropriate now to observe further what the prophet means by a servant. The Old Testament conception of a servant is one who does work for a master in complete submission to the will of that master — in our language, a slave. However, the submission of a Hebrew slave was not forced submission, but rather willing submission. A man might be the unwilling slave of another (in order to pay a debt, etc.) for six years and no more. At the end of that time he was free. Nevertheless (says Exodus 21:5, 6), "If the servant shall plainly say, I love my master . . . I will not go out free: Then his master shall bring him to the judges; he shall also bring him to the door, or unto the door post; and his master shall bore his ear through with an aul; and he shall serve him for ever."

Our Lord did not have to become a "slave." He was the Lord of glory. But the Father wanted a slave to rescue lost humanity. So the Son of God in his love for His Father (and our Father) and for us, went to heaven's door, as it were. There, in a figure, His ear was bored through and He became Jevovah's Servant "forever."

Now of all the qualities to be desired in a servant the most important is complete submission to the master's will. The master receives no benefit from a disobedient slave. Willing obedience, however, was the kind given by a Hebrew slave, for he did not have to be a slave. So it was with Jesus. He was the willing servant of Jehovah. Of Him the Psalmist writes: "I delight to do thy will, O my God: yea, thy law is within my heart" (Psalm 40:8).

In these verses before us our Lord is most fully shown in His servant, or slave, character — utterly dedicated to His Master's will no matter how unpleasant the course to which it takes Him. His submission led Him to suffering, death, and burial. Once He took the "form of a servant," as Paul says, then there was no avoiding "death, even the death of the cross" (Philippians 2:7, 8).

Our text shows Him first submissive in his *suffering* (verse 7); then submissive in His *death* (verse 8); and finally submissive in His *burial* (verse 9).

Our attention is now directed to

THE SUBMISSION OF THE SERVANT IN HIS SUFFERING
(verse 7)

"He was harassed and belabored, yet did he not open his mouth; and as a sheep to the slaughter he was led, yet as a ewe before her shearers is tongue-tied so did he not open his mouth."

1. The Treatment Unjust

The utter injustice of the treatment men gave our Lord on the night and day of His passion is seen in the words "harrassed"* and belabored." I translate them thus because they show (as the Hebrew indicates) how our Lord was literally "pushed around" from one mocking trial to another, and then to an-

*A form of the Hebrew word is translated "taskmaster" (Exodus 3:7) and to "exact a debt" or to levy a tax (Deuteronomy 15:23; Daniel 11:20).

other and another. Only law-breakers deserve such treatment as this. He was scourged by Pilate (John 19:1) in fulfillment of this prediction. But beatings are for the intractable and rebellious. These things are for evil men. Jesus was a good man. He was obedient to every ordinance of man. He who deserved the praise of all men and the protection of the law received the abuse of all and the wrath of the law.

2. The Response Submissive

Now most of us know how we would react in such circumstances. We, with our Anglo-Saxon tradition of trial by jury and the presumption of innocence until proven guilty, would not have taken this "sitting down," as we say. Yet Jesus did. He was utterly unprotesting — "yet he did not open his mouth."

Isaiah now brings before us two illustrations of this submissive behavior.

Like a Sheep Going to Slaughter

"As a sheep to the slaughter he was led."* Though many of my readers have never seen this done, it was a familiar sight in our Lord's land and time. Twenty-five years ago when cold storage facilities did not make it easy for farmer-folk to have fresh meat in warm weather, our meat was mostly

---

*Compare Jeremiah 11:19 and Job 10:19, where the same Hebrew word is used.

cured pork or fresh poultry in the summer-time. So, often at the time of harvest when my mother was cooking for from five to fifteen harvest hands my father used to kill a yearling wether for meat. The animal would be separated from the herd (western American sheep go in "herds" not "flocks" and the men who tend them are "sheepherders" not "shepherds") and led to the place of slaughter (usually the hay derrick). He might be carried or led, but was seldom driven. Beating simply has no effect on a sheep to cause it to go in a desired direction. Yet never once did I ever hear one of these lambs for the slaughter utter any noise of protest. This is the way our Lord went.

Like A Ewe at her Shearing

"Yet as a ewe before her shearers is tongue-tied so did he not open his mouth." Sheep-shearing has been a task on farms from time immemorial. Jacob, David, Absalom, and many other Biblical characters appear in connection with sheep-shearing. Even today there are hundreds of men in western North America who shear sheep in Mexico in late winter and then move northward during the spring months till in early summer they have finished for the season somewhere in northern United States or in Canada. Yet, there is one thing no sheep-shearer in the last 5000 years has heard — a sheep protesting over the fact that it is being fleeced, any more than the butcher has ever heard a sheep protest over being slaughtered. I have seen the sheep gouged, scratched, cut, and bruised in the hands of callous-hearted shearers whose only goal was to shear as many sheep as possible in a day. They often come bleeding from the shearing shed. The knife may slice the throat; the shears may slash the sides, but the most one hears is a kind of subdued sigh through the nostrils. Even a coyote or sheep-killing dog arouses no cries from the flock. The sheep can express hunger and thirst, or a frolicking mood, but it just simply does not or cannot express vocal protest at mistreatment. One need only contrast this with the nature of a hog to see how unusual this is. A hog will squeal to the last drop of blood in his body when he is being slaughtered. Be thankful pigs do not have to be sheared!

Our Lord might have "squealed like a pig" — if it is not too shocking even to contemplate the thought — and that justly. But He did not. He came not to live; He came to die in the sinner's place. This was the Father's will.

On the other hand, think what a heart-rending recollection it will be for a restored and repentant Israel when they remember all this and confess the things recorded in the first six verses of this chapter.

It is true that others have "walked the last mile" with silence and self-composure. Even fallen men have enough remmant of the image of God left in them to control their feelings at times. But no one ever walked that "mile" willingly as Jesus did. No other ever did it with His motives. Why? Because no one else ever had a divine mission such as His and such willing submission to the divine will.

The gospel records portray exactly how Jesus fulfilled this prophecy. He groaned, He called on God; but to Herod, Caiaphas, Pilate, and all the rest, He answered not one word of protest.

Now the subject moves on to another aspect of our Saviour's submission—

THE SUBMISSION OF THE SERVANT IN HIS DEATH
(verse 8)

"From confinement and from judgment he was snatched away; and among his contemporaries who did consider that he was cut off from the land of living ones; on account of the transgression of my people, the stroke was his?' "

Owing to the highly emotional character of this passage and the obscurity of certain of the words, almost every phrase of this verse is a subject of disputed interpretation. The interested reader may observe in the footnote the reasons given for my own translation*

*Every clause of this verse, almost every word, has been a matter of dispute among learned men. Proposed translations follow.
"He has been taken away from prison and from judgment: and of

The confession of Israel appears now to be at an end. Throughout these three verses the speaker appears to be the prophet himself.

Will the reader note five different specifications about the death of our Lord, to which his submission led Him.

1. Circumstances of His Death

Note first the *circumstances* of His death. "From confinement and from judgment he was snatched away." "Taken" is altogether too tame a word to describe what happened. The Hebrew word describes hurried, forcible, violent treatment, resulting in death. This is the word of Ezekiel when he says (Ezekiel 33:4) "the sword come, and take him away." How well this describes the treatment Jesus received in those early morning hours when the Jews hurried Him from Gethsemane to trial and then to

---

His generation who considered 'He was snatched away out of the land of the living; for the wickedness of my people punishment fell upon Him'?" (F. Delitzsch)
"From distress and from judgment he was taken; and in his generation who will think that he was cut off from the land of the living, for the transgression of my people as a curse for them?" (J. A. Alexander)
"Hurried was he from prison and judgment; His posterity who shall declare? For He was cut off from the land of the living, For my people's transgressions was stricken." (F. C. Jennings)
'By tyranny and law was he taken And of his age who reflected, That he was wrenched from the land of the living, For my people's transgressions the stake was on him?" (George Adam Smith)

execution, without any of the ordinary just processes of law! They wanted to get Him out of the way before the Passover. Thus in the midst of hate, violence, and physical force our Lord's last hours were spent.

2. Scene of His Death

Note secondly, the *scene* of His death. It was "prison and judgment" or as we have rendered, "con finement (or detention) and . . . judgment." Detention, or confinement, describes, I think, the arrest in the garden and the continued detention throughout the day. "Judgment" is here the word for judicial proceedings. How swiftly events moved that night and day! After His arrest He went through at least five trials of a sort. There was first the interrogration of Annas, then the mocking thing in the high priest's

---

"After arrest and sentence he was taken off, And on his fate who reflected?" (C. R. North)

"He was taken away from prison and from judgment: and among his contemporaries who was concerned? For he was cut off out of the land of the living: for the sin of my people he was taken away; and as for his generation, who *among them* considered that he was cut off but of the land of the living for the transgression of my people for whom the stroke *was due?*" (American Standard Version)

"He was taken from prison and from judgment: and who shall declare his generation? for he was cut off out of the land of the living: for the transgression of my people was he striken." (Authorized Version)

The poetical and emotional character of the passage and the unusual usages of words characteristic of such literature in all languages added to the difficulty. The following observations may aid the interpreter who knows Hebrew in handling the passage.

palace before the Sanhedrin (Matthew 26:57 - 66). Next, there was a short hearing before Pilate (Matthew 27:1, 2). After that He appeared before Herod (Luke 23:11-26). There was hardly a shred of legality to a single one of the trials. He was in a high priest's palace, in Herod's chambers, and in Pilate's judgment hall. These were the scenes where the "tender mercies of the wicked" were conferred upon Him on that last sad day.

3. Heart-Break of His Death

In the third place, note the *heart-break* of the situation — "And among his contemporaries who did consider?" "Generation" in the Authorized, which

---

1) ואת before *doro* is to be taken in the sense of "and with respect to." This is the use of the form in Numbers 3:46 ("and with respect to the redemption of" etc.). Brown, Driver, and Briggs list about 45 cases in which this is the significance of את or ואת

2) *Ki* before *Nigzar* is to be taken as introducing direct discourse, as is indicated by the first person suffix on עם (people). Such is a very common use of *ki*, about the equivalent of אותי in Greek (See Genesis 21:30, Exodus 21:30, cf. Luke 4:21).

3) *Lamo* may be either *le* with the suffix third, masculine, singular or *le* with the suffix third, common, plural. However, it is evidently third, masculine, singular here as in Isaiah 44:15 — the equivalent of *lo* (to him). The antecedent of this pronominal suffix is the Servant.

Thus, a translation is determined somewhat similar to that of Delitzsch, and except for the second clause, similar to the Authorized Version. "He was snatched away from confinement and from judgment; and as for his contemporaries who considered: 'he was cut off from the land of living ones; on account of the transgression of my people was the stroke his?.' "

I have translated "contemporaries," refers to the people of His own time. Who, of his own time and nation, asks the prophet, pondered or realized what was going on? The answer is "Few or none." Nobody cared that His character was holy and His treatment unjust, or that our Lord was worthy honor instead of dishonor. And, sorrow of sorrows, nobody cared, as the last part of our verse informs us, that the real purpose of His mission was to take the stroke of divine wrath for the very people who were killing Him. From John the Baptist onward (John 1:29) He had been declared to be the Lamb of God who was to take away the sin of the world. But the attitude of the world then was the same as it is now — So what?

4. Nature of His Death

In the fourth place, see the nature of the death He suffered — "he was cut off from the land of living ones." What does it mean to be cut off? It is said in II Chronicles 26:21 that when King Uzziah became a leper "he was cut off from the house of the Lord." This means that he was excluded from the temple. In like manner, death excluded Jesus from the scene of life and association with living people. Jesus was God, but because He was also man, He could die, just as all men can die. It was to become capable of dying as a man that the incarnation took place (Hebrews 2:9). What is it that makes death a fearful thing? I do not think it is so much the pain. It is rather the fact that death erects a barrier which excludes the dead forevermore (except for the resurrection) from fellowship with living people. All our happiness is connected with the scenes of life and with association among living people. Death puts a stop to all this. Jesus experienced this kind of separation from the scenes of life and of living people. Death for Him was no less a tragic experience than it is for all mankind.

5. Purpose of His Death

Finally, our text reveals the *purpose* of that death. It was "on account of the transgressions of my (that is, Isaiah's) people the stroke was his." From one view this is the cause of His death. But, ignoring the technicality, it is clear that His one main purpose was to suffer the divine wrath in the sinner's place. He took the stroke, the passage says. This is the usual way to express a divine visitation of punishment. It is used of the plagues of Egypt and of the leprosy of Uzziah. There is a stroke which was due us. It was the infliction of an endless Hell. Thank God the stroke has already fallen — fallen upon Christ.

Now, will you consider what they would not — that the circumstances of His death were violent, hurried, forcible treatment for the meek and mild Jesus; that the *scene* of His death was the garden of unlawful arrest and the halls of five rigged trials; that the special *heart-break* of His death was the utter carelessness of all the people of His own nation on that day He died for their benefit; that His death was *real,* the same grim separation that is for all men; and that the *purpose* was vicarious — to die in our stead?

How often the theme of substitution appears in this "golden passional," as Polycarp called it! It is no wonder the hymn writers make much of it.

The agonies of Calvary,
    Could not His love dismay;
He would not yield, tho' God revealed
    The price that He must pay.

He stood condemned in Pilate's Hall,
    He heard the rabbles' cry;
The King with none to own His cause,
    My cause would not deny;

Lo, Jesus stands with broken heart,
    With nail-pierced hands and feet;
He points unto His cross of woe,
    Where love and mercy meet.

The Savior stands at thy heart's door
    Bruised for thy cruel sin;
Oh why not open wide the door
    And let Him enter in?

The story of our Lord's submission concludes with

THE SUBMISSION OF THE SERVANT IN HIS BURIAL
(verse 9)

"And there were those who appointed his grave with the wicked ones; yet he was with a rich man in his deaths,* because he had done no violence and there was no fraud in his mouth."

The Authorized Version has led its readers entirely astray as to the meaning of the first part of this verse. It reads, "And he made his grave with the wicked." The American Standard Version has corrected this with the reading: "And they made his grave with the wicked." Also, I think the sense of the passage demands that "and with the rich in his death" should be changed to "but he was," etc. The first clause describes what some wicked people wanted; the second what really happened.

Our Lord's submission to God and man was such that had there been no overruling providence He would have endured not only an unjust suffering before death, and then unjust execution, but a shameful burial in potter's field, as well, Observe the facts.

1. The Burial Plans of Wicked Men

---

*The Hebrew word is plural, probably indicating immensity or intensity, as is common in certain nouns.

Wicked men did plan a shameful burial for the Saviour. "There were those who appointed his grave with the wicked." This translation is fully sustained by the Hebrew, as to sense, if not quite as to terms. The simplest, and, I think, most natural understanding of the Hebrew words bears out that "those who appointed his grave with the wicked" were His own "contemporaries" mentioned in the preceding verse.

I think it is obvious that nothing would have given the cruel and venal men who caused our Lord to die greater pleasure than after having killed Him to bury Him in a public dump-ground among the graves of criminals, prostitutes, and the abandoned men of old Jerusalem's "Skid Row." Surely, it would have brought pleasure to Satan, the arch-fiend of them all. Nothing is said about this in the gospels, but there is no reason to doubt that those who caused Jesus to be executed as a criminal expected Him to be buried as one. It would have been the normal thing*

But there is a God in heaven, who brings the counsels of the wicked to nought. Wicked men might plot to let the dogs gnaw the bones of the Son of God

---

*Josephus (*Antiquities of the Jews*, Book IV, Chapter VIII, 6), in commenting on the laws of his people writes," He that blasphemeth God let him be stoned, and let him hang upon a tree all that day and then let him be buried in an ignominious and obscure manner."

and to expose His flesh to the buzzards before committing His remains to a shallow hole in the city dump. Travellers tell us that in that region the bodies of executed criminals are often allowed to be eaten of beasts and birds. A number of Biblical figures of speech presuppose the custom. But long before, God had said He would not permit His Holy One to see corruption (Psalm 16:10). This could not be if wicked men were to have their way to the end.

2. The Burial Plans of a Righteous God

Such consecration as Christ's would not go unrewarded. So we read that God appointed Him a grave with a "rich man." Matthew tells us that on the day of the cruficixion "When even was come, there came a rich man of Arimathea, named Joseph, who also himself was Jesus' disciple: He went to Pilate, and begged the body of Jesus. Then Pilate commanded the body to be delivered. And when Joseph had taken the body, he wrapped it in a clean linen cloth, And laid it in his own new tomb, which he had hewn out in the rock: and he rolled a great stone to the door of the sepulchre, and departed" (Matthew 27:57 - 60).

3. Why God Overruled

The final section of verse nine presents the reason for this remarkable divine overruling. It was "because he had done no violence, and there was no fraud in his mouth."

Our Lord was right in His deeds. He was not a violent man. Neither was He guilty of "wrong," "unrighteousness" or "injustice," as the word is sometimes translated (Genesis 16:5, Exodus 23:1, Job 16:17). These things our Lord had not done even once. In Him for the first time in history the words of Psalm 1:1, "Blessed is the man that walketh not in the counsel of the ungodly, nor standeth in the way of sinners, nor sitteth in the seat of the scornful" became fully applicable to any one man. This verse of ours (Isaiah 53:9) is prophetic witness to the sinless walk of Christ Jesus 700 years before He was born. His own testimony (John 8:46) and that of Pilate, (Matthew 27:24; Luke 23:14, 15); Pilate's wife, (Matthew 27:19); the Centurion, (Matthew 27:54); the repentant thief, (Luke 23:41); and the apostles (I Peter 2:22) bears it out. No one has ever risen to meet His challenge to convict Him of sin.

The Lord was also right in His thoughts. "And there was no fraud in his mouth." He was neither deceived nor deceitful. He never spoke a lie, simply because it was not in His heart to speak one. In the words of Psalm 32:2, "In his spirit there was no guile," and in a sense far higher than it could have been true of Nathaniel, He was "an Israelite, indeed, in whom is no guile." He could ascend into the "hill of the Lord" and "stand in his holy place" because He had "clean hands, and a pure heart." He is one "who hath not lifted up his soul unto vanity, nor sworn deceitfully."

The reason, then, for our Lord's being saved from the shame of a criminal's grave was that His humble submission to the will of God throughout His life earned it for Him. Treatment of the corpse had nothing to do with atonement. His death accomplished that. After the soldier's spear was thrust into His side, wicked, violent men were not allowed to touch Him again. To the flood of Jewish spite and hate God said "No!" "Thus far and no farther."

Two Important Observations

Before we leave these precious verses I call attention to two things.

Precision of Prediction

There is no place in all prophecy (with the possible exception of the eleventh chapter of Daniel) where the precise and detailed prediction of future events followed by precise and detailed fulfillment is so clearly in evidence. The pursuit into the garden, the arrest, and the unresisting behavior of Jesus are predicted in verse seven. The trials, the unnecessary violence of the captors, their utter lack of concern, and the substitutionary death apear in verse eight.

Verse nine is the most specific of them all— predicting such an unlikely event as the fact that Jesus, executed on conviction of blasphemy, was saved from shameful burial according to the Jewish custom, through the request of Joseph, who begged His body from the Roman governor and buried it in his own new tomb. The Lord was, indeed, "with a rich man in his death."

A Lesson in Submission

Finally, for Christians, there is a lesson in holy behavior taught by example, a lesson which the writers of the New Testament have not missed. Peter, in addressing some remarks to "Servants" who, he said, were to be subject to their masters, uses the submissive behavior of the great "Servant of Jehovah" as an example, and in doing so he addresses the following admonition to us all.

"Servants, be subject to your masters with all fear; not only to the good and gentle, but also to the froward. For this is thankworthy, if a man for conscience toward God endure grief, suffering wrongfully. For what glory is it, if, when ye be buffeted for your faults, ye shall take it patiently? But if, when ye do well, and suffer for it, ye take it patiently, this is acceptable with God. For even hereunto were ye called: because Christ also suffered for us, leaving us an example, that ye should follow his steps: who did no sin, neither was guile found in his mouth: Who, when he was reviled, reviled not again; when he suffered, he threatened not; but committed himself to him that judgeth righteously: Who his own self bare our sins in his own body on the tree, that we, being dead to sins, should live unto righteousness: by whose stripes ye were healed. For ye were as sheep going astray; but are now returned unto the Shepherd and Bishop of your souls" (I Peter 2:18 - 25).

May God help us, who not only have reaped the judicial benefit of Calvary in the forgiveness of sins but also a blessed example in suffering persecution, to learn the same submission to God and the same obedience to His will. May it be said of us, truly, as Tennyson put it, "Our wills are ours to make them thine."

CHAPTER FIVE

The EXALTATION of the Servant of the Lord Isaiah 53:10-12

> Yet Jehovah pleased to crush him; he did make him sick. When his soul shall place a trespass offering, he shall see posterity; he shall prolong days; and the plan of Jehovah shall succeed in his hand.
>
> Because of the travail of his soul he shall see; he shall be satisfied by his knowledge.* My righteous servant shall procure righteousness for the many, since he himself bears their punishments.
>
> Therefore I will allot to him a portion among the mighty; and with the powerful he shall divide gain; because he bared his soul to the death, and with transgressors he was numbered; and he himself lifted up the sin of many, and made intercession for the transgressors.

---

*This division of thought, connecting "by his knowledge" with "he will see" first occured to me in preparation for a lecture to my Hebrew students in 1945 or 1946. And I presented the translation thus for several years. I observe that Dr. North, as does also H. Wheeler Robinson (*The Cross in the O. T.*, p. 64), favors this translation in his work of 1948, quoted and cited frequently in the appendix to this book (*op. cit.*, p. 126). Though not fully supported by the Massoretic accents it does find support in the Septuagint and is fully justified by the consonantal text.

This "Golden Passional" now closes as it began—with the voice of Jehovah God the Father It began, "Behold my servant shall act wisely; he shall be exalted; he shall be lifted up, and shall be very high." Now it closes with the description of the concluding acts of His wise activity and of the rise to glorious exaltation, which Jehovah had said would result.

Summary

Others have spoken in the meantime. A repentant and restored Israel has poured forth a confession of past hostility for the Servant, followed by criticism, then late pity, finally succeeded by repentance and faith in Him as their reconciling substitute. Their words fill verses one to nine. Then the prophet, himself, speaks briefly in verse 10 and part of 11. Finally, Jehovah himself brings it all to a solemn but thrilling climax in the last verse and a half.

Up to this point the benefits of the Calvary work of Christ have all been presented from the standpoint of the redeemed. He has suffered for their transgressions; He had borne their punishments; He has taken their stripes; He has healed their wounds. Now, another point of view is taken. We learn what God the Father and Christ the Son have received and will yet receive in benefit from Calvary.

All ages past — all ages future — all look with one face toward that mysterious event when — riddle of riddles, mystery of mysteries — God the Creator died for man the creature's sin! The Lamb "slain from the foundation of the world" is also the one about whom the redeemed shall lift their paeons of praise forever.

Prospect

Our text now describes the final issue of the "sufferings of Christ" in "the glory which should follow." But, before doing so, it draws our attention to the basic "formal cause" of His sufferings. That cause was the plan of God. Our common version says, "It pleased the LORD to bruise him. . . ." I cannot accept fully the sense of this translation.* Commentators have labored hard to find a pleasure for the Father in the crushing of the Son. In my opinion, the cup must have been as bitter for the Father as for

*Four facts seem to make it clear that the divine plan and purpose are in view rather than divine enjoyment. *First*, the position of *Jehovah* is emphatic in the sentence. Usually the verb is first in Hebrew clause, but here the subject, Jehovah Himslf is first. This indicates that Jehovah's activity is to be declared. *Second*, the meaning of *chaphets* ("it pleased" A. V.) specifies will or purpose quite as often as mere pleasure (e.g., Judgmes 13:23). Third, the voice of the verb is active, not passive ("pleased," or "purposed" — not "was pleased"). *Fourth*, and most important, the sentence structure seems to require this sense, for "Jehovah pleased" is followed by an infinitive (Kal construct infinitive of דכא) with a pronominal suffix in accusative relation. This us-the Son. Jehovah was delighted at His Son's willingness to die (as His witness at the baptism, Matthew 3:17, proves), but not at the fact of death itself. This "pleasure" of God is the same plan of God that Paul mentions as the "good pleasure of his will, . . . his good pleasure which he hath purposed in himself . . . according to the purpose of him who worketh all things after the counsel of his own will" (Ephesians 1:5, 9, 11).

Jehovah plan to crush His Son? you ask. Yes, He did. Before He made us, when earth and sky and man and beast were only thoughts in the mind of God, He planned to do so (I Peter 1:20). Calvary was no accident, no improvisation in the "nick of time." In that first Christian sermon, on the first day of Pentecost after the death of Christ, Peter reminded his Jewish audience that "Him, being delivered by the determinate counsel and foreknowledge of God,

---

ually expresses purpose of some kind. A parallel case of this grammatical construction indicating purpose with chaphets (pleased) is Job 23:32.

Besides these grammatical facts, there is evidence from other Scripture. The Bible clearly teaches that God did plan from eternity to bruise the Son (I Peter 1:20; Acts 2:23).

Learned and devout men of the past have labored hard to explain this fact and to relate it to the divine foreknowledge. The results of their cogitations have not been in agreement. It is the opinion of this writer that this is one of the facts of God's truth that we are to accept by faith as true and to wait for God in heaven to explain.

ye have taken, and by wicked hands have crucified and slain" (Acts 2:23).

Yet, the crushing of His Son was for the ultimate greater glory of that Son — and this we see in the words of our text to follow concerning the exaltation of the Servant of Jehovah to prosperity, to satisfaction, and to compensation for His labor.

THE EXALTATION OF THE SERVANT TO PROSPERITY

(verse 10)

"When his soul shall place a trespass offering, he shall see posterity; he shall prolong days; and the plan of Jehovah shall succeed in his hand."

1. The Cause of the Servant's Prosperity

The cause of God's Servant's success or prosperity is said to be the fact that His soul shall place a trepass-offering. The word "when" with which this statement is introduced is about the equivalent of "because" or "since." This indicates that the making of the trespass-offering is the cause of His prosperity. A learned commentator has suggested that the entire clause should be rendered that His soul shall transform itself into a trespass-offering. This is exactly what happened in the case of our Lord. His soul,* that

*The word "soul" (*nephesh in Hebrew*) deserves special treatment. It has 46 different translations in the Authorized Version. Usually translated "soul" it frequently serves much like psyche, "soul" in

is, the life, which the Scripture says was in the blood, became a trespass-offering. There were five main offerings in the Mosaic dispensation. The trespass-offering is the last treated in the main description of them in Leviticus one to seven. It spoke of one aspect of atonement that none of the others did. That aspect was restitution. The distinctive feature of the ceremony was that it was accompanied by restitution for wrongs committed against the holy procedures of the Mosaic Law (Leviticus 5:16, 6:4). It was presented "to make amends for the harm that he hath done" (Leviticus 5:16).

At any rate, before it could become a trespass-offering, the animal had to be slain. So it was that Jesus became our trespass-offering, not only dying to bear all our punishments but also at the same time paying to God every debt we owed Him. He is not only our propitiation but also our satisfaction before God.

---

the New Testament. It is predicated of both men and beasts. Thus it refers to the animating principle of the body (Genesis 2:7) and includes all its emotions and appetites (Proverbs 23:2, Ecclesiastes 6:7, Numbers 21:15). To this life principle the blood is mystically connected. Girdlestone (*Synonyms of the Old Testament*) says: "In Hebrew, as in most languages, the shedding of a man's blood was a phrase used to represent the taking of his life, for 'the blood is the life.' In this oft-repeated phrase (e. g., Leviticus 12:11, 14) we see that the blood is (i. e., represents) 'the soul;' and if the one flows out from the body, the other passes away too. In Proverbs 28:17, we read literally, 'The man that doeth violence — to the blood of a soul shall flee into the pit:' so in Ezekiel 33:6, Jonah

2. The Elements in The Servant's Prosperity

There are three elements in the Servant's Prosperity.

A. Numerous Offspring

The first is descirbed in the words "he shall see posterity." To a Hebrew one of the most obvious evidences of the Lord's blessing and of real prosperity was a large family of children. Contrariwise, it was regarded as stark tragedy for one to die childless. This chapter was written first for Hebrew readers, and here was one real evidence of their Messiah's future success — He was to have numerous offspring. A close look at the context will show that the very scene of childbirth is in the background — but let us wait for the next verse before pursuing this thought. Just this much now: it was "when his soul" makes itself a trespass-offering—when He was dying — that He caught a vision of His offspring. I do not insist upon it, but it seems to me that this must be in the

---

1:14s... This mystical identification of the blood and the life is of great interest as bearing on the work of Christ. We are told that He poured out His soul unto death and that He shed His blood for the remission of sins. Evidently the shedding of the blood was the outward visible sign of the severance of the soul from the body in death, and this severance is regarded as a voluntary sacrifice offered by the Divine Son, in accordance with His Father's will, as the means of putting away sin."
There are other Hebrew words similar in meaning to *nephesh,* (soul). The commonest are *ruach,* usually "spirit," and *chayyah,* usually

background of such a passage as Psalm 22:30 which, after predicting the sufferings of Christ says, "A seed shall serve him; it shall be accounted to the Lord for a generation." Another is Psalm 45:16, which says of the coming Lord and King that "Instead of thy fathers shall be thy children, whom thou mayest make princes in all the earth."

B. Long Life

The second element in His prosperity is to be great length of life. The words are: "he shall prolong days." Great length of life, as among all peoples, was among the Hebrews of Isaiah's time regarded as evidence of God's favor. Long life was promised for obedience to parents in "the first commandment with promise" (Exodus 20:12), as a reward for honest dealings (Deuteronomy 25:15), and to the son who kept the commandments of the Lord (Proverbs 3:2). In Jesus' case it was almost an insoluble mystery for the three days between His death and resurrection that God would give Him

---

"life." The first, "spirit," answers to the Greek pneuma. It refers usually to the higher nature of man, which corresponds to the nature of God. God is *ruach* (spirit) in the Old Tesament, but not *nephesh* (soul). The word *chayyah* (life) is close to *nephesh* (soul) in meaning.
There is no general rule for consistent translation. Hebrew psychology and anthropology operated in different categories from ours. Old Testament scholarship cannot agree at the present time on important aspects of the problem though warm scholarly warfare continues.

"length of days." But, the resurrection morning solved the mystery. This explains the Apostolic claim that His resurrection was "according to the Scriptures."

C. Successful Accomplishment

The third aspect of the Lord's prosperity is indicated in the common version by the words, "and the pleasure of the Lord shall prosper in his hand." As we showed earlier in this chapter, the words "please" and "pleasure" here refer to the plan of God. When Jesus came, God committed the accomplishment of a plan into His hand. That plan, as set forth in the first chapter of Ephesians and in other passages, was to accomplish the redemption of a fallen world by His death in the sinner's place. "Jehovah pleased (planned) to crush Him." Our verse says that His plan "prospered," or as the Hebrew literally means, it "came to completion" in His hand. From the moment He declared that He "must be about my Father's business" on past the time when He formally dedicated Himself to the death at His baptism and when He firmly set His face to accomplish His decease at Jerusalem, He never wavered. The devil tried to kill Him as a babe and keep the Father's plan from coming to completion; at least three times He was tempted by Satan to throw it over; His mother at the Cana wedding feast tried to get Him to abortively manifest Himself thus to avoid the conclusion of His task; Peter tried to talk Him out of it, yet He fought the thing through in the garden of Gethsemane, and finlly, after five or six hours of cruel pain on the cross, He cried, "It is finished." *Tetelestai!* It is finished! The payment of the price of our redemption was finished. His course was finished. The Old Testament Law was finished. The typology was finished. One of the gospel writers might have truthfully added that then another Old Testament prophecy was finished too — that "the plan of Jehavoh shall come to completion in his hand."

The next verse tells of

THE EXALTATION OF THE SERVANT TO SATISFACTION
(verse 11)

"Because of the travail of his soul he will see;* he shall be satisfied by his knowledge. My righteous servant shall procure righteousness for the many since he himself bears their punishments."

Commentators have wrestled for centuries with the problem of how the Lord justifies men "by his knowledge" as indicated in most versions. My translation, which is fully justified by the Hebrew,* joins the words "by his knowledge" with his satisfaction rather than with His procurement of righteousness

*See note on first page of this chapter.

(justification) for the many. I think it is the correct translation

1. The Figure of Child-Birth — The Cause of Satisfaction

The figure in the verse, half veiled by the stately language, is the scene of childbirth. Such is the meaning of the "travail."

Several times now I have been present at the scene of childbirth. From what I have observed, as well as by the testimony of a family physician, I know that at the time a mother travails and is delivered of her offspring she is much refreshed in spirit when the sight of her babe meets her eyes. There is a light kindled in her eyes and a joy of accomplishment.

Our Lord went through travail, the travail of bringing into existence a spiritual "seed" at Calvary. His pangs were such as no mother ever knew. His were of "his soul." It had its seat within the personality rather than merely in the body. It had its voice in the words of Gethsemane, "My soul is exceedingly sorrowful, even unto death," and in those other words from the cross, "My God! My God! why hast thou forsaken me?"

In that awful hour He had a vision — "Be cause of the travail of his soul he shall see." The word is that used of the prophetic visions of the Old Testament prophets, as well as of natural sight. This one was prophetic— prophetic of the "many sons" He would yet bring into glory.

Best of all, says our prophet, when He was to have the vision, "he shall be satisfied by his knowledge." What did He know? He knew that the ones for whom He had just prayed (John seventeen) — the disciples and all those who should believe on Him through their spoken and written testimony down through the present age — would come trooping into glory. He saw the redeemed of all ages, saved by His grace, bought by His blood, sanctified by His Spirit, glorified in His presence, safe in heaven's portal — past the pearly gates. The knowledge gained by such a vision was surely satisfying to Him.

2. The Element in Satisfaction

I have been anticipating a bit, for in the last half of the verse the elements involved in His satisfaction are delineated before us. A learned student of this passage (Geo. Adam Smith) has translated it as follows: "My servant, righteous himself, wins righteousness for many, and makes their iniquities his load."

His satisfaction, then, was that He undertook successfully to provide righteousness for His many spiritual seed, and that by assuming their sin's penalty He was able to see at the moment of victory the teeming fruit of His travail.

Note that to do this He had to be "righteous himself." To take the sinner's place there could be no sin of His own commission.

He had to "win righteousness for the many." This He could do, for once our sins were imputed to Him, His righteousness could be imputed to us (II Corinthians 5: 17-21; Romans 3:24-30).

Oh, there is a real peace and joy in knowing a Saviour like this — one whose satisfaction consists in making the burdens of sinners His load. Paul said his glory was the cross. Long before Paul's day, Jeremiah wrote (9:23), "Thus saith the LORD, let not the wise man glory in his wisdom, neither let the mighty man glory in his might, let not the rich man glory in his riches: but let him that glorieth glory in this, that he understandeth and knoweth me, that I am the LORD which exerciseth lovingkindness, judgment and righteousness, in the earth: for in these things I delight, saith the LORD."

> In the cross of Christ I glory,
> Tow'ring o'er the wrecks of time;
> All the light of sacred story
> Gathers round its head sublime.
>
> When the woes of life o'er-take me,
> Hopes deceive, and fears annoy,
> Never shall the cross forsake me;
> Lo! it glows with peace and joy.

When the sun of bliss is beaming
Light and love upon my way,
From the cross the radiance streaming
Adds more luster to the day.
Bane and blessing, pain and pleasure,
By the cross are sanctified;
Peace is there that knows no measure,
Joys that thro' all time abide.

Finally, this great oracle closes with

THE EXALTATION OF THE SERVANT TO COMPENSATION (verse 12)

"Therefore I will allot to him a portion among the mighty; and with the powerful he shall divide gain; because he bared his soul to the death, and with transgressors he was numbered; and he himself lifted up the sin of many, and made intercession for the transgressors."

As in the two verses preceding, the Lord presents both the causes for the Servant's exaltation and the elements involved in it. This time, however, the order is reversed and the causes are saved till last. It is as if God would not close on the theme of the Servant's exaltation without one more reference to the atonement, even more precious than the exaltation.

1. The Elements in Compensation

A. A lot among the Mighty

The compensation our Lord receives for His service is described, first, as receiving a lot among the great. "Therefore, I will allot to him a portion among the mighty." The very word for "allot" signifies the division of the fruits of victorious battle. When the Israelites had conquered a large section of Canaan, Joshua superintended an allotment of it among the twelve tribes — and this is the very word used for the division. David used the same word in referring to division of spoil among his men after victory over the Amalekites.

And who are the mighty ones with whom He will share the fruits of victory? They are the same as those referred to in verse eleven as "the many" who are justified. "Mighty ones" and "many " are the same Hebrew word and probably refer to the same group. So, together, the Lord and His saints shall "possess the kingdom."

What is the inheritance allotted? I think it is that group of "kings" and "many nations" introduced in 52:13 as utterly confounded over the final glory of Christ as His coming and kingdom. David prophesied of this saying, "Ask of me, and I shall give thee the nations for thine inheritance, and the uttermost parts of the earth for thy possession" (Psalm 2:8). Psalm 72:8-11 tells how "He shall have dominion also from sea to sea, and from the river to the ends of the earth. They that dwell in the wilderness shall bow before him; and his enemies shall lick the dust. The kings of Tarshish and of the isles shall bring presents: the kings of Sheba and Seba shall offer gifts. Yea, all kings shall fall down before him: all nations shall serve him."

B. Gain among the powerful

About the same thought is presented in the second statement, "And with the powerful he shall divide gain." Who are these "powerful" ones? There can be small doubt that they are the armies of the redeemed, of whom Psalm 110:3 says, "Thy people are thorough devotion in the day of thy power." These are the armies who follow Him on white horses (Revelation 19:14) and who go forth to destroy Antichrist and his false prophet, whose bodies are committed to the "burning flame." They are confessing Him now; He will confess them then.

2. The Causes of the Servant's Compensation

Yet, all this, remember, is *His* victory. He is the one who is able to open the seals to the "title deed to the universe" and breaking those seals hears the redeemed sing "a new song, saying, Thou art worthy to take the book, and to open the seals thereof: for thou wast slain, and hast redeemed us to God by thy blood out of every kindred, and tongue, and people, and nation; And hast made us unto our God kings and priests: and we shall reign on the earth" (Revelation 5:9, 10).

One ought really to speak for an hour or to write a whole book to treat these last four statements of the prophecy.

Why is He worthy of such compensation? Because —

"He bared his soul to the death."* Not like some slavish gladiator did He go to the arena, driven by whip, or like Bryant's quarry slave, "scourged to his dungeon," but voluntarily He went. He bared His own life to the cruel cross in self-dedication. "I lay down my life," said He. "No man taketh it from me, but I lay it down of myself. I have power to lay it down, and I have power to take it again" (John 10:17, 18). And it was to "the death." It was "even the death of the cross." It was *the* death of all time. "Time's tragedy" was in the Saviour's heart that day, not in the "aching stoop" of Markham's "Man With the Hoe."

---

*A startling recent interpretation of Philippians 2:8, the famous "kenosis" passage, is that Paul had in mind these words, "he hath poured out his soul unto death" and was referring to the death of Christ rather than to his incarnation. (See *The Cross in the Old Testament,* H. Wheeler Robinson, pp. 104, 105.) Arguments in support are quite convincing. This interpretation of Philippians 2:7, *heaouton ekenosen*) was set forth in *Theologisches Worterbuch zum Neuen Testamentum* (ed. G. Kittel, Stuttgart 1952) in the article "*Pais Theou*". It has since been translated into English as *The Servant of God* by W .Zimmerli and J. Jeremias. No. 20 in *Studies in Biblical Theology* (Alec R. Allenson, Inc., 625 East Ogden Avenue, Naperville, Ill.)

"And with transgressors he was numbered." The mythology of a corrupt Christendom has numbered Jesus among the saints. False religion has numbered Him among the prophets. But God and the Jews numbered Him with transgressors — common thieves — on that fearful day. Even He Himself numbered Himself among them, for on the last night He told Peter, "I say unto you, that this — that is written must yet be accomplished in me, And he was reckoned among transgressors: for the things concerning me have an end" (Luke 22:37). What bitter but blessed fulfillment that saying had! The "end" of which He spoke arrived when they crucified Him between two thieves.

"And he himself lifted up the sin of many." The scape goat, over which Aaron confessed the sins of the people and which carried those sins away to the wilderness, comes before us now. What that animal did in symbol Jesus did in actuality. He lifted up our sins and carried them all away. How joyously Peter echoes this statement: "Who his own self bare our sins in his own body on the tree, that we, being dead to sins, should live unto righteousness: by whose strips ye were healed" (I Peter 2:24)!

The prophecy closes with the statement, "And (He) made intercession for the transgressors." "Intercession" here means essentially to strike or to assail something. Thus, one receives the impression of the

Son of God assailing the throne of His Father on behalf of transgressors. The Hebrew also indicates that this intercession is a work that has now been begun, but, unlike the finished work prophesied in the three statements with which it is parallel, it is still going on. This intercessory ministry began long before the end of our Lord's earthly life and is seen in pathetic but majestic operation in Gethsemane and in the so-called high-priestly prayer of John seventeen. The most striking fulfillment of the prophecy is in the prayer "Father, forgive them: for they know not what they do," made while still hanging on the cross (Luke 23:34). When one considers that every saint is a saved transgressor, this prayer takes on a still wider perspective. The ministry of intercession continues in the glory where according to Hebrews 7:25 "he ever liveth to make intercession" for them "that come unto God by him." And the mind turns from that to another precious reminder of this fact: "It is Christ that died, yea rather, that is risen again, who is even at the right hand of God, who also maketh intercession for us" (Romans 8:34).

Conclusion

Only God Himself could have devised a message like this oracle set in the fifty-second and fifty-third chapters of Isaiah. Only God could have made known the facts herein revealed.

We have heard this marvelous prophecy. God's Servant is first presented as the submissive Servant destined to both suffering and glory — destined to be gaped at by many people at His first coming on account of the baseness of His humiliation, destined to be gaped at again on account of the marvel of His glory at the second coming. Then we have heard a repentant Israel confess that the one whose message and person they once rejected and crucified for sins which they thought His own was really their promised Messiah, slain for their own sins. Just now we have heard the prophet and Jehovah speak of His destined glory. How accurate, how precise, how detailed the prophecy is both in prediction and fulfillment.

As I bring these expositions to a close, I can find no words better fitted to express my feelings than those with which Albert Barnes closed his remarks on this passage over 100 years ago. A century of time has not detracted one whit from the pungent pertinency of his words.

"This whole chapter is exceedingly important to Christians. It contains the most full, continuous statement in the Bible of the design of the Redeemer's sufferings and death. And after all the light which is shed on the subject in the New Testament; after all the full and clear statements made by the Redeemer and the Apostles; still, if we wish to see a full and continuous statement on the great doctrine of the atonement, we naturally recur to this portion of Isaiah. If we wish our faith to be strengthened, and our hearts warmed by the completion of his sufferings, we shall find no part of the Bible better adapted to it than this. It should not only be the subject of congratulation, but of much fervent prayer. No man can study it too profoundly. No one can feel too much anxiety to understand it. Every verse, every phrase, every word should be pondered until it fixes itself deep in the memory, and makes an eternal impression on the heart. If a man understands this portion of the Bible, he will have a correct view of the plan of salvation. And it should be the subject of profound and prayerful contemplation till the heart glows with love to that merciful God who was willing to pour out his soul unto death. I bless God that I have been permitted to study it; and I pray that this exposition—cold and imperfect as it is—may be the means yet of extending correct views of the design of the Redeemer's death among his friend, and of convincing those who have doubted the truth of the Bible, that a prophecy like this demonstrates that the Book in which it occurs must be from God."

CHAPTER SIX

The IDENTITY of the Servant of the Lord Isaiah 40-53

Not long ago a young woman, a graduate student at a large mid-Western university asked the writer for help on a problem related to the subject of this book. As she explained it, the problem was part of a story in which she herself was involved.

This is the story. In her classes she became friendly with a young man pursuing a course of study similar to hers. Being a sincere Christian believer, she sought to witness to the man and to present the gospel to him. He was a professed unbeliever in any "revealed" religion, no friend of Christianity. So she persuaded him to read the stories of our Lord's betrayal, suffering, and death in the Gospels and likewise the prophecy of Isaiah 52:13-53:12. This young woman had no technical theological training; therefore, she tried to do no more than let the prophecies of Isaiah and their New Testament fulfillment tell their own story and do their own work in the young man's heart.

They did their work. He was quite convinced and was about to take steps to become a professing Christian.

But he decided to take the matter to one of the professors in the religion department of the university — a department which happens to be the theological seminary of a large Protestant denomination. By this professor he was told that the prophecies of Isaiah really refer to the people Israel, that their similarity to the events in the career of Jesus of Nazareth is quite co-incidental.

At the time the young woman reported this to me her friend had been diverted, at least temporarily, from his decision to become a Christian.

Now, the lady wanted to know, was there something I could tell her which might help in dealing further with the man, and was there some literature which they could read? Happily there was something to say and literature to read as well.

The story points up several pertinent facts. First, it exemplifies the sort of treatment that Isaiah's prophecy now receives at the hands of many modern Biblical scholars. Though now treated with more respect than a couple of generations ago, that it is a valid prediction of events in the career of Jesus is not allowed by many leading technical Biblical scholars. This is true in spite of the fact that for the first seventeen or eighteen centuries of Christian history hardly a voice was raised against it in all Christendom. Naturally this was never the Jewish interpretation, though there are several varieties of Jewish Messianic interpretation of Isaiah 53.

Second, it shows that the passage is valuable in strengthening the faith of those truly born again, as well as quite convincing to unbelievers. The young woman's faith did not waver and the young man was at least brought further toward faith in Christ than he ever had been before.

Third, the story shows what really ought to be plain enough anyway — that faith and unbelief can never quite be made compatible. Either the professor or the girl is right. To accept the one conclusion leads to faith in Christ as Saviour of the world; to accept the other leads to rejection of Him. To say that Isaiah was uttering timeless truths about the redemptive power of innocent suffering, which the New Testament has applied to Christ, without at the same time recognizing, as Jesus did, that "Thus it is written, and thus it behoved Christ to suffer" (Luke 24:46) may seem to be a good compromise. But such a message would never have convinced the young man in question that he ought to say as Peter: "Thou art the Christ, the Son of the living God." Nor would such a mild conviction have compelled the first evangelists to proclaim boldly and convincingly that "Christ died for our sins according to the Scriptures" (I Corinthians 15:3).

Finally, does this incident not suggest that some examination of this passage, in context, should be made, to see what the contextual basis of a Messianic interpretation may be?

The New Testament has settled for believers the question of whether or not the prophecy of Isaiah 52:13 - 53:12 speaks of Christ. The larger question is, Does this passage speak exclusively of Him? And there is a still more important question: Do all the portions of Isaiah which describe the Lord's servant have Jesus Christ as their subject?

On account of the fact that the great prophecy of our Lord's career in Isaiah 52:13 - 53:12 is broken apart by the chapter division, the designation "servant" for Christ at 52:13 is commonly unknown, though it reappears in 53:11. This is further complicated by the fact that New Testament references to this designation cite the Septuagint (early Greek) translation *pais,* which in turn is rendered "child" rather than "servant" in the Authorized Version. This is corrected in more recent versions. As a result, it is only in technical or semi-technical discussions, as a rule, that "the servant of Jehovah" is related to this passage.

The references to the Lord's Servant are numerous in Isaiah. The references to the servant in 52:13

and again in 53:11 happen to be the last two of a series, beginning at 41:8, of references to the servant of the Lord. All of the last major division of Isaiah (chapters 40-66) is devoted to a message of comfort to Israel in view of the coming captivities and other national disasters.*

Students of all persuasions have always marvelled at the literary excellence of this latter portion of Isaiah, no less than at its spiritual depth. Into the portion lying in chapter 41 through chapter 53 is woven a series of mysterious references to the Servant of Jehovah. Among these are four portions often designated by scholars as "songs" of the Servant. In strange, even cryptic fashion, various speakers are introduced in the so-called songs. These songs are usually limited to 52:1-4; 49:1-6; 50:4-9; and 52:13-53:12.

---

*The scope of this book does not allow a discussion of the question of the date and authorship of this portion of Isaiah. With the advent of the "age of reason", criticism has progressively divided up the authorship of Isaiah into, first, two main writers and, since the publication of a commentary by a German named Bernhard Duhm (*Das Buch Jesaia* Goettingen, 1892, 1901, 1914, 1922) into three. Chapters 1-39 are said to be generally authentic, the work of Isaiah the son of Amoz in the eighth century B. C.; chapters 40-55 by a man of the sixth century B. C.; chapters 56-66 the work of a contemporary (perhaps a disciple) of the second but continuing on somewhat later. Mighty pens have been raised in defence of the unity and authenticity of the whole of Isaiah. Recent strong defences in the English language and easily accessible are *The Unity*

REFERENCES TO THE "SERVANT" IN ISAIAH 40-53

The reader is urged to trace carefully through the following survey of this section of Isaiah, wherein the idea of the Servant of the Lord is developed. The passages must be allowed to speak for themselves as to the identity of the Servant, the nature of His career, and His significance. Really one ought to read in his own Bible the whole of these chapters for himself for, several commentaries notwithstanding, the Servant references are an integral part of a lengthy context. For the sake of brevity, however, and more as an introductory survey of the subject than as a full discussion of it, the procedure will be to discuss mainly the actual verbal references to the Servant.

Having predicted the future salvation of Israel from all enemies by the coming of very God himself (40:10), the prophet first mentions the servant in these words: "But thou, Israel, my servant, Jacob whom I have chosen, the seed of Abraham my friend, thou whom I have taken hold of from the ends of the earth, and called from the corners thereof, and said unto thee, Thou art my servant, I have chosen thee and not cast thee away; fear not thou, for I am with thee" (Isaiah 41:8-10).

---

of Isaiah. O. T. Allis (The Presbyterian and Reformed Publishing Co., Philadelphia) and *An Introduction to the Old Testament* and *Studies in Isaiah,* Edward J. Young (Eerdmans, Grand Rapids).

That the servant of the Lord in this passage is Jacob, or Israel, is a certainty. The plain sense of the words makes no other interpretation possible.

The next explicit reference to the servant is at 42:1-7. The first four verses constitute one of the so-called servant songs, which some recent critical scholarship discerns; the second paragraph seems clearly to refer to the servant, and it is difficult to tell where to end the paragraph. Inasmuch as this is a very important passage and a distinct step in the development of thought, it is now cited in full.

"Behold, my servant, whom I uphold; my chosen, in whom my soul delighteth; I have put my Spirit upon him; he will bring forth justice to the Gentiles. He will not cry, nor lift up his voice, nor cause it to be heard in the street. A bruised reed will he not break, and a dimly burning wick will he not quench; he will bring forth justice in truth. He will not fail nor be discouraged, till he have set justice in the earth; and the isles shall wait for his law.

"Thus saith God Jehovah, he that created the heavens, and stretched them forth; he that spread abroad the earth and that which cometh out of it; he that giveth breath unto the people upon it, and spirit to them that walk therein, I Jehovah, have called thee in righteousness, and will hold thy hand, and will keep thee, and give thee for a covenant of the people, for a light of the Gentiles; to open the blind eyes, to bring out the prisoners from the dungeon, and them that sit in darkness out of the prison-house" (Isaiah 42:1-7).

Two facts stand out in the first paragraph. The first is that the servant of the Lord is to have a mission to "bring forth justice to the Gentiles." Opinion has somewhat divided as to whether this is as a prophet, as a priest, or as a ruler of some sort. But in any case a second fact is plain — that the Lord's servant is a person. There is disagreement, but most recent criticism is agreed on this. Certainly the lay reader would hardly come to any other conclusion.

In the second paragraph a third fact, related to the first, is set forth — the servant is to provide salvation for the Gentiles. Whether this salvation is of some natural physical sort or spiritual is not absolutely clear, but the language is most naturally taken in a spiritual sense.

It should be emphasized that in this "song" the servant is a person. This is granted by leading advocates of most views. Delitzsch has said: "The servant of Jehovah who is presented to us here is distinct from Israel, and has so strong an individuality and such marked personal features, that the expression cannot possibly be merely a personified collective" (*Commentary* Vol. ii, p. 174).

Now at 42:18-20 comes a startling variation in the theme: "Hear, ye deaf; and look, ye blind, that ye may see. Who is blind but my servant? or deaf as my messenger that I send? who is blind as he that is at peace *with me*, and blind as Jehovah's servant? Thou seest many things, but thou observest not; his ears are open, but he heareth not." Whoever the servant is, he is something of a failure, in this text. Evidently though closely allied with the Lord (he seems to be a prophetic messenger of God) he fails even to understand his message. This is quite in contrast to the previous predictions of a successful mission to the world (42:1-7).

At 43:10 it appears that there is a group of messengers called God's servant (singular) and that the essential knowledge which the blind servant should have imparted was the "Mosaic" monotheism of the burning-bush revelation (Exodus 3), *viz.* "Ye are my witnesses, saith the LORD, and my servant whom I have chosen: that ye may know and believe me, and understand that I am he: before me there was no God formed, neither shall there be after me."

Next appear three clear references to the servant as Israel, "Yet now hear, O Jacob my servant, and Israel, whom I have chosen; Thus saith Jehovah that made thee, and formed thee from the womb, who will help thee: Fear not, O Jacob my servant; and thou Jeshurun, whom I have chosen" (Isaiah 44:1,2). These two references identifying the servant with Israel are immediately followed by promise of an outpouring of the divine Spirit upon the thirsty Israelites — obviously a great spiritual blessing of some kind (cf. 44:3-5). There is a latent suggestion that the blessing is to extend to all mankind, much as in the promise of the outpouring at Joel 2:28 ff., which in the New Testament is given application to the church's baptism in the Spirit at Pentecost (Acts 2:16 ff). It is of interest that "Jeshurun," a poetical name for Israel, first appearing at Deuteronomy 32:15, meaning "the upright one," is used here. In the context of the effusion of the Spirit such a meaningful name is most appropriate. At verse 21 is the third of these references wherein it is affirmed that the servant, Israel, shall not be forgotten of God.

As a prophet (or prophets) the servant next appears in the famous Cyrus prophecy. This portion, wherein the name of Cyrus, king of Persia, is announced by a prophet who lived over a century before Cyrus was born (granting that it is unusual), presents no serious problem to those who believe in predictive prophecy. The enormous literature on this passage can only be noticed here; what is important to this discussion is that in connection with this Cyrus prediction "the word of his (Jehovah's) servant" is presented in synonymous parallel with "the counsel of his messengers" and that in connection with poetic discourse on the validity of the predictive message of the Lord's prophets. The pertinent words are:

"Thus saith Jehovah . . . that confirmeth the word of his servant, and performeth the counsel of his messengers: that saith of Jerusalem, She shall be inhabited . . . that saith of Cyrus, He is my shepherd . . . " (44:24-28).

Before proceeding further in this recital, observe that the servant of the Lord has appeared first as Israel, then as a Saviour of the Gentiles, after that as an uncomprehending, inefficient messenger of God to the world, and now distinctly as a prophet foretelling the restoration of Jerusalem under the leadership and authority of Cyrus the king of Persia. This is the Cyrus known as "the Great" because he overcame the Babylonian Empire and replaced it with his own in and following the year 538 B. C.

The next three references to the servant are as "Jacob my servant" (45:4), "his servant Jacob" (48:20), and "my servant, O Israel" (49:3).

Now there comes a definite advance. The servant is no longer Israel, as such; no longer a saviour of the Gentiles, as such; nor is he a prophet, as such. He is set forth as the saviour of Israel. Here are the words: "And now saith Jehovah that formed me from the womb to be his servant, to bring Jacob again to him, and that Israel be gathered unto him (for I am honorable in the eyes of Jehovah, and my God is become my strength); yea, he saith, It is too light a thing that thou shouldest be my servant to raise up the tribes of Jacob, and to restore the preserved of Israel: I will also give thee for a light to the Gentiles, that thou mayest be my salvation into the end of the earth" (Isaiah 49:5, 6). The reader will now have noticed that in the first of these two verses the servant claims that Jehovah has commissioned him "to be his servant, to bring Jacob again to him." In the second, the servant elaborates the claim; "thou shouldest be my servant to raise up the tribes of Jacob, and to restore the preserved of Israel."

These claims of the servant make it impossible to regard him simply as the people Israel. Rather, in the light of the previous context, he is an Israelite who is to become the effective and successful restorer of his countrymen.

It is significantly added that the servant will not only restore and save Israel but that he is to become "a light to the Gentiles, that my salvation may be unto the end of the earth."

The next pertinent portion of Isaiah is 50:4-9. By the nearly unanimous consent of recent commentators these verses are to be regarded as a kind of song or poem recited in the first person by the Lord's servant, even though mention of the servant, as such, does not appear. The portion is immediately followed by an address of the prophet to the followers of the servant.

"The Lord Jehovah hath given me the tongue of them that are taught, that I may know how to sustain with words him that is weary: he wakeneth morning by morning, he wakeneth my ear to hear as they that are taught. The Lord Jehovah hath opened mine ear, and I was not rebellious, neither turned away backward. I gave my back to the smiters, and my cheeks to them that plucked off the hair; I hid not my face from shame and spitting. For the Lord Jehovah will help me; therefore have I not been confounded: therefore have I set my face like a flint, and I know that I shall not be put to shame. He is near that justifieth me; who will contend with me? let us stand up together: who is mine adversary? let him come near to me. Behold, the Lord Jehovah will help me; who is he that shall condemn me? behold, they all shall wax old as a garment; the moth shall eat them up.

"Who is among you that feareth Jehovah, that obeyeth the voice of his servant? he that walketh in darkness, and hath no light, let him trust in the name of Jehovah, and rely upon his God" (Isaiah 50:4-10).

This passage is the closest parallel to 52:13-53:12 in these earlier servant portions. The servant is one who is fully obedient to the Lord's will and commission and, seemingly as a consequence of such obedience, must submit also to smiting, plucking off of hair, shame, and spitting by wicked men (see especially verse 6).

Next, and finally, there comes the most lengthy section of all, Isaiah 52:13-53:12, wherein details of the servant's coming career are set forth with special reference to his suffering in his people's stead and his subsequent exaltation and final glory. No further attention will be devoted to this final portion at this point, inasmuch as it is the subject of the main body of this book.

Christian Interpretation of Isaiah 52-13 - 53:12

Since the very earliest times of which there is record (and our record happens to go back to the very day of the foundation of the Christian church), there has been one uniform Christian interpretation of the fifty-third chapter of Isaiah: The servant is Jesus Christ, the man of sorrows who gave His life at Calvary for the sins of the world. Naturally, opinions have differed as to the precise identity of the servant in the earlier passages noted above. And there have been many varieties of interpretation of the minutiae. The general "Christological" frame of interpretation, however, has always prevailed in Christian circles. Even in the earlier passages (Isaiah 42:1 ff. for example), it has always been the usual

Christian view that these verses attain complete fulfillment only in our Lord.

It is probable that the Messianic interpretation of Isaiah 53 was not new when Jesus and the early Christians expounded it. For, among the Aramaic paraphrases of the Old Testament called targums is one (Targum of Jonathan ben Uzziel) which identifies the servant in Isaiah 42:1, 43:10, and 52:13-53:12 as Messiah. Scholars think these targums were first oral only and underwent revision from time to time. But, they received most of their present bulk in the last five centuries B. C. Jonathan ben Uzziel, who is said to have reduced this oral targum to writing, was a disciple of Hillel of the first century B. C. Even if a third or fourth century A. D. date for the final editing of this targum is correct, as certain scholars assert, it is hardly conceivable that the Jews would have first begun to use this interpretation after the Christians had used it to prove that Jesus of Nazareth was the Messiah. The "personal Messiah" interpretation has, however, survived among Jews till the present. One form of their interpretation reported in the Babylonian Talmud supposes that there will be two messiahs, one to suffer and die, a second to resurrect the first. There is evidence also that the Jewish sect of Qumran, now known to us through the Dead Sea Scrolls and other recent finds, gave Isaiah 53 a Messianic interpretation.

A survey of Christian opinion certainly ought to begin with the New Testament. It is exceedingly probable that the first witness in importance therein is that of the Father God. At Jesus' baptism His voice was heard saying: "This is my beloved Son, in whom I am well pleased" (Matthew 3:17). Mark reports the saying as: "Thou are my beloved Son, in thee I am well pleased" (Mark 1:11). These words are a conflation of Psalm 2:7, "Thou art my son" and Isaiah 42:1, "in whom I am well pleased" or as the version has it, "in whom my soul delighteth." These words of the Father Himself constitute the first New Testament testimony that the servant of Isaiah's prophecies is Jesus Christ. One could hardly ask for a greater. C. R. North has written that these words were probably heard by Jesus only, and at a later time communicated by Him to the disciples. He thinks it inconceivable that the disciples or the evangelists had the insight to invent these words (*The Suffering Servant in Deutero - Isaiah* p. 25).

Probably the aged Simeon, whose blessing on the infant Jesus is reported by Luke, should also be mentioned. He quite evidently interpreted the prophecy of the servant at Isaiah 49:6 as relating to Jesus (see Luke 2:29-32).

John the Baptist is a third witness. When Jesus came to him, he exclaimed, "Behold, the Lamb of God, that taketh away the sin of the world" (John

1:29). There is not strict verbal correspondence, but scholars of many persuasions agree that the author of these words was thinking of Isaiah 53:4, 11. Some will claim that the author of the fourth Gospel put these words in John's mouth. But even if that be granted (which we certainly do not grant), it clearly represents a very early Christian interpretation of Isaiah 53.

That Jesus Himself so interpreted the servant passages is likewise clear. There is specific proof of this at Luke 22:37, where Jesus is reported to have said: "For I say unto you, that this which is written must be fulfilled in me, and he was reckoned with transgressors: for that which concerneth me hath fulfillment." The Scripture to which He refers is Isaiah 53:12. On another occasion, when Peter, James, and John were questioning about his death and resurrection, Jesus asked them, "How is it written of the Son of man, that he should suffer many things and be set at nought?" (Mark 9:12). Isaiah 50:6, "I gave my back to the smiters, and my cheeks to them that plucked off my hair; I hid not my face from shame and spitting" as well as the whole of Isaiah 52:13-53:12 must have been the writings to which he referred — not to say that the similar prophecies at Zechariah 12:10 and even others (Psalm 22) may not also have been in His thought. Incidentally, some early Christians accepted the crucifixion of Jesus between two thieves as fulfillment of Isaiah 53:12, for somehow Mark 15:28 came into the text of the New Testament at a very early time. "And the scripture was fulfilled, which saith, And he was numbered with the transgressors" is the way this verse reads. Though now properly rejected as a spurious text, not present in the original manuscript, it was added at a very early time, for several uncial manuscripts as well as several ancient versions contain it. The consciousness of Jesus that He was to die for the sins of "many" (Mark 10:45; 14:24 cf. Isaiah 53:11) must certainly have been shaped by Isaiah's prophecies, as well as His firm conviction that the time of His death by crucifixion was to be his "hour" (Mark 10:41; Luke 12:50; John 12:23, 27; 13:1). One of the leading recent authorities in Old Testament theology, not a conservative, has written that Jesus Himself must have shaped His mission in the light of these passages and that the disciples found in them the only unquestionable and sufficient basis for the faith that Christ died for our sins "according to the Scriptures" (H. Wheeler Robinson, *The Cross in the Old Testament*, p. 101).

The New Testament writers and evangelists received Isaiah's servant prophecies as predictions of Jesus Christ. Matthew reports Jesus' kindly healing ministry and self-effacing public approach and then claims these as fulfillment of Isaiah 42:1 ff. (Matthew 12:17-21). A better-known example is the case of Philip, who preached Jesus to the Ethiopian eunuch by way of explanatian of Isaiah 53:7 ff. (Acts 8:27-39). Repeatedly the sermons and prayers of the early chapters of Acts refer to Jesus as the Servant. This is obscured by the Authorized Version (1611) which erroneously translates this word as "child." The Greek word is *pais,* used regularly by the Septuagint (Greek translation of the Old Testament used in our Lord's time) to translate ' עבד the Hebrew word for servant in Isaiah. *Pais* does sometimes mean child, but it obviously cannot be so meant in these passages in Acts. These references in Acts are 3:13, 26; 4:27 and 30. Note that in the same context (Acts 4:25) David as a prophet is called God's *pais* (servant). It is close to certain that Paul is alluding to Isaiah 53:11 in his statement that "through the obedience of the one shall the many be made righteous" (Romans 5:19). Finally, Peter's description of the suffering Jesus (I Peter 2:22-25) is a paraphrastic application of Isaiah 53 to the passion of our Lord, showing how Peter felt about this matter.

The New Testament teaches, then, that "Christ died for our sins according to the scriptures" (I Corinthians 15:3) and that among the most prominent of these Scriptures are the predictions of the Lord's servant in Isaiah 41-53.

As far as Christian interpretation of the servant prophecy of Isaiah 53 is concerned, it can be stated that no other interpretation than this Messianic one was ever seriously entertained during the first seventeen centuries of the Christian era. A number of extensive studies of the history of interpretation on this point have been conducted in the last several decades and none known to this writer reaches a conclusion different from this. One of the most thorough and authoritative works reports that during the subapostolic and patristic periods the Messianic interpretation of Isaiah 53 was unchallenged. Occasionally someone might apply a Servant portion to a prophet (eg. Chrystostom's view of 50:4-9), but on chapter 53 opinion was united on the Messianic interpretation. Reformation days did not develop any change, adds Dr. North, and when the heretic Servitus maintained that Isaiah 53 referred to Cyrus it only showed that he was truly a miscievous person (North, *op. cit.* p. 26).

Alternatives to the Christian Interpretation of Isaiah 52:13 - 53:12

As suggested above, while Christian interpretation of Isaiah 52:13-53:12 has been uniformly Messianic, there has been some variety of interpretation of other servant portions of Isaiah. Non-Christian interpretation, however, has been far from uniform.

These statements reflect our point of view that any interpretation which rejects the clear testimony of the New Testament is not a Christian interpretation, whatever the personal faith of the man advocating it may be. This is not simply pronouncing *anathema* on those who disagree. It is simply to recognize that rejection of the New Testament and uniform Christian concensus is to reject Christianity itself. It is, of course, possible to set forth a new religion in which reason is substituted for revelation and ethical teaching for salvation and to call that religion Christianity, but any informed Christian ought to protest against such unfair manipulation.

It should be pointed out that once the historical and doctrinal witness of the New Testament is laid aside and the unity of Scripture denied or ignored, there really is no way of knowing who the servant of Isaiah is. If we cannot know for sure that the events ascribed by the New Testament to the career of Jesus of Nazareth really occurred or that the words ascribed to Him were really spoken, then how can any correlation be made between prediction of Christ and fulfillment? The New Testament is the only reliable source we have for the life and words of Christ. It should not surprise the reader, therefore, to learn that alternatives have generally been proposed by those who take low views of the New Testament. It is somewhat reasurring to learn that even the most advanced radical criticism is having a hard time these days justifying second-century second-hand sources for the New Testament.

The first alternative view to be noted is that

1) *the servant is the people Israel.* This is the most common Jewish interpretation. Let the world-renowned aged Dr. Joseph Klausner, Professor Emeritus of Hebrew Literature and Jewish History at the Hebrew University of Jerusalem, furnish his opinion. He claims that "just as the prophet suffers without having committed a fault, suffers from the transgressors among his own people whom he is seeking to benefit, that is to say, *takes upon himself the iniquity of others,* so suffers also the people Israel from other peoples more sinful than Israel, because Israel seeks to benefit them. In other words, *the people Israel takes upon itself the iniquity of all the rest of the peoples, the iniquity of the whole world.* What the prophet is to Israel, Israel becomes to all the world: the servant of the LORD, holding up the standard of the Highest righteousness in the world and suffering for his pursuit of good. This is the profound conception that lies hidden in 42:1-7; 49:1-9; 50:4-9; 52:13-15 plus 53:1-12" (*The Messianic Idea in Israel, pp.* 161, 162).

Klausner claims that some of the career of Jesus did resemble that described in Isaiah 53 and that "the rest of his career is *intentionally* portrayed in the Gospels in such a manner that the events appear to have happened in fulfillment of the words in this chapter" (*Ibid*).

Klausner's further remarks indicate that he believes that the passage is messianic in the sense that the "elect of the nation gradually became the Messiah of the world, the redeemer of mankind" (*Ibid*, p. 163).

This comprehensive view regards the servant then as progressively inclusive of the entire nation of Israel, the prophet and his associates, and finally the spiritual (elect) of the nation.

This view may be found in whole or in part in Jewish circles throughout most of the Christian era. Since the coming into Christian circles of anti-supernatural higher criticism of the Bible, this view in almost all particulars has been the most common "higher critical" interpretation.

Actually, it must be recognized that there is some truth in it, for any fair view will have to recognize a place for Israel and the prophets. The tragic aspect of it is the categorical rejection of Jesus Christ and of the historical value of the New Testament.

That the servant has certain prophet characteristics and a prophetic mission, in part, is quite certain. But no prophet fits even a major portion of the particulars. The exaggeration involved when the magnitude of the servant's mission to save both Jews and

Gentiles, to die for "all" etc., is viewed is simply too enormous to be granted. This would be beyond hyperbole. If the servant were the prophet-author of the prophecy, he would even be guilty in certain portions of having God describe him as the saviour of the world. It is inconceivable that any Hebrew prophet could ever have done that.

2) *The Servant is a prophet.* This theory is suggested by several expressions in the servant passages, and at least once the servant is a messenger (or messengers, 44:26). Since the seventeenth century there have been a few interpreters who thought the servant to be Jeremiah, who in chapter 53 is typical of Messiah. In the late eighteenth century and in the nineteenth century, before ideas of a second Isaiah became widespread, Isaiah himself was sometimes suggested. An unknown prophet or even the whole order of prophets was likewise suggested. It was inevitable that when Isaiah 40-66 became regarded as a separate work (or works) from chapters 1-39 and treated as the work of an author (or authors) of the late sixth (and fifth) century, a century and a half later than Isaiah the son of Amoz, the so-called "Deutero Isaiah" himself should be claimed as the servant. This "autobiographical" interpretation has the support of several recent authors.

This view also fails to meet the requirements of the context of Isaiah. To avoid these difficulties, it has assumed many forms. Yet to the present moment, even in the "collective interpretation" form of Eichrodt, Robinson and other contemporary and near contemporary writers, satisfactory adjustment to the requirements of context has not been made.

The chief contextual objections to the Israel and prophet interpretations follow in summary form.

a) Israel appears as the cause of the Servant's sufferings. In 53:4-6 Israel confesses that it is "our griefs . . . our sorrows" that He bears. This excludes the possibility that the *nation* as a whole is the servant.

b) In chapter 53 the Servant suffers in order that the "many," presumably the confessing Israelites, go free from that suffering. Now if the nation as a whole be the servant, this creates the impossible situation of Israel's being both the sufferer and the ones free from suffering — in the same sense. If it be said that the servant is the elite (elect spiritual minority) then there is another problem, *viz.* historically, the spiritual minority of Israel and the carnal majority both suffered alike in the nation's calamities. Ezekiel and Daniel go into captivity to suffer. Jeremiah stays at home to suffer. All three minister to disobedient Jews who likewise suffer.

c) There are several passages where the servant's characteristics and activities are so distinctly personal that only an individual single man could hardly be intended. These distinctly personal features are especially prominent in the four servant songs: 42:1-4; 49:1-6; 50:4-9, and 52:13-53:12. In the first song the gentleness and patience ascribed to the servant are charactistics of a person, rather than of a group. In the second the inner subjective reaction to apparent failure is "personal reassertion of a challenged faith" (H. Wheeler Robinson). He cries. "I have laboured in vain, I have spent my strength for nought, and in vain: yet surely my judgment is with the LORD, and my work is with my God." What could be more personal than this and more unlikely as a group reaction? In the third there are both outer and inner characteritics of a single person. As to the outer: he speaks of his tongue, his ear, his cheeks, and of his hair—and that all in the first person. As to the inner: he speaks of personal communion with God, of his willing response to God's will and of his own submissive reaction to mistreatment by fellowmen. In the fourth song (and here the reader is referred to the many details set forth in the five main chapters of this book) we have the distinct sketch of the career of one man.

When one reflects on the details of the "portrait" painted by these four songs, observing their coherence, harmony, and complementary force, he must admit that they most naturally fit the face of only one man—

a man whom one might recognize if one were to meet him and become acquainted with him. Christians have always seen that face in the Gospel portrait of Jesus of Nazareth.

d) There is no suggestion anywhere in the prophecies of the servant that Isaiah means anything but the nation as a nation when he refers to Israel. It is pure assumption to identify him with the disciples of a prophet or the pious minority.

e) The servant has a mission to Israel which is certainly hard to explain if the servant is the community of Israel. That he is the spiritual minority who save the community is eliminated on the above grounds.

The scholarly reader will do well to examine North's arguments against the collective theory of the "corporate personality" school (*op. cit.* 205-207).

North's penetrating comment on the intrinsic difficulties of all forms of this view is appropriate here.

"If, however, it is difficult to affirm that the whole of Israel was the Servant, it is attractive, on *a priori* grounds, to suppose that the Servant was the godly Minority within Israel. No theory appears antecedently so reasonable, and the beginner is apt to accept it at once. It seems to make the best of both worlds. But when we come to delimit or qualify, where are we to stop? It would seem that we are at once on an inclined slope, and that there is no arresting the process of being carried down until we touch bottom with the admission that what we have in the Songs 'is essentially an individual experience' " (*op. cit.* pp. 202, 203).

3) That *the servant is an historical person* of civic, religious, or even of supposed messianic im portance has been suggested by various and numerous writers. The recent survey by C. R. North (*op. cit.*), pronounced "masterly" and praised for "completeness of detail" by H. H. Rowley (*The Servant of the Lord*, p. 3), presents no less than nine such interpretations besides the different prophets suggested. Hezekiah and Uzziah, two contemporaries of Isaiah, have been proposed. A supposed Meshullam was suggested not long ago by an author who equates an obscure word translated "he that is at peace" (42:19) with the proper name of the servant. This author further identifies the servant with the Meshullam who is the elder son of Zerubbabel (I Chronicles 3:19). Zerubbabel, Jehoiachin, Ezekiel, and Cyrus are contemporaries and near contemporaries of the supposed "Second Isaiah" who have been proposed. Even the name of Moses has been seriously advocated. Actually, as most will agree, the very variety of historical identifications shows how tentative and unsatisfactory all of them really are.

Occasionally someone has proposed that

4) *The servant is a personified ideal.* He is (or it is) an ideal kind of man drawn after the pattern of some noble historic or contemporary sufferer. This theory is entirely wanting in evidence of context.

Finally, mention must be made that since the beginning of the twentieth century there has been a view that

5) *The servant is a mythological figure* whose pattern has been imported from some of Israel's neighbors. At an earlier stage of this line of interpretation certain radical critics supposed him to be a Hebraized sort of nature god that in Babylonian mythology is Tammuz, who died and rises again like the cycle of life and death in the seasons of the year. More recently it has been suggested that the suffering servant is a Hebrew reconstruction of a similar dying Baal in the mythology of Canaan, as seen in the Ugaritic literature (Ras Shamra tablets).

Besides these many distinct varieties of interpretation, there have been many ingenious efforts at synthesis of several views. Indeed, the nature of the facts almost precludes any simple explanation relating all the data to some one single person or idea.

It is interesting to note that one scholar, Ernest Sellin, successively advocated in scholarly writings four different theories — identifying the servant with

Zerubbabel, with Jehoiachin, with Moses, and with "Third Isaiah."

For those acquainted with the literature of the subject of Biblical prophecy there is no necessity to demonstrate that there really are only two important bases for rejection of the Christian interpretation: in the case of the Jewish interpreters, rejection of Jesus of Nazareth as the Jewish Messiah; and in the case of the others, rejection of or doubt of the possibility of super-natural, divinely imparted knowledge of remote future events. It is no accident that the non-Jewish objections to the Christian view have arisen in the modern period. The same period of history in Christendom and the same forces which produced deism and other denials of the possibility of the supernatural have produced these naturalistic interpretations of Scripture. Even writers who show evidence of sincere personal faith in Jesus Christ as the divine Saviour of the world are to be found raising thoroughly naturalistic objections to the traditional Christian Messianic interpretation of Isaiah 53. This seems to be the case with Dr. North, whose valuable work has been several times cited herein. It is beyond the scope of this little book to discuss the philosophical and apologetical issues involved. This has been very adequately done by Dr. O. T. Allis in his book *The Unity of Isaiah* (The Presbyterian and Reformed Publishing Company, Philadelphia, 1950. The title is slightly misleading, for it is really a systematic defense of the valid predictive nature of important sections of Bible prophecy and should be read by every person seriously interested in this subject.

It should be added that if one's presuppositions do not allow him to accept predictive prophecy as a possibility, then evidence is useless. However, if his mind is open on the subject, this writer is confident that he will be greatly impressed by the facts of which this book is an exposition, and God willing he will be convinced and converted.

Christian Messianic Interpretation

No apology is necessary for boldly advocating a Christian Messianic interpretation. It has been sufficiently demonstrated to be the New Testament view of the major servant prophecies of Isaiah. The further duty remains of explaining this view and of adjusting it to clear statements in the Isaiahan context to the effect that the servant is Israel, a prophet, or some other entity.

I would remind the reader that, as seen earlier, two major portions of the servant prophecies are specifically said in the New Testament to be prophecies of Jesus Christ. These are the long section of Isaiah 53 and an important portion of chapter 42. This is not to say that no reference to some other person or to a group of persons may not likewise be encompassed in some parts of the servant prophecies. That would be to ignore the comprehensive, organic character of many Old Testament predictions. It does mean that these prophecies point ultimately and *of divine intention* to Christ — that these are real predictions. And, in the case of the fifty-third chapter, at least, I think it can be safely claimed that we have prediction that points directly and exclusively to Him.

Many students have observed that there is a comprehensive grasp of the future — sometimes also of the past — in some prophecies that includes many events of a similar or related kind, which are nevertheless widely separated in time. Many names have been given to this feature — the most objectionable being "double fulfillment." Franz Delitzcsh, a renowned Jewish-Christian German scholar of the second half of the nineteenth century, spoke of it as the "apotelesmatic" character of prophecy.

J. A. Alexander, a somewhat earlier nineteenth-century American scholar, without naming this feature spoke of it somewhat obliquely as follows: "All prediction, or prophecies in the restricted sense, are not specific and exclusive, i. e. limited to one occasion or emergency, but many are descriptive of a sequence of events which has often been realized" (*Isaiah Translated and Explained,* vol. 1., p. 14).

Albert Barnes, a contemporary of Alexander, whose scholarly works on the original text of Isaiah,

Daniel, and Job deserve fuller study than has ever been given them, wrote very clearly and most satisfactorily on this subject. His extensive introduction to Isaiah (*Notes on Isaiah*, vol. I) will reward the industrious reader. Of this feature he states: "This is not double sense; it is *rapid transition* under the laws of *prophetic suggestion*" (*Ibid.*, p. xlix).

Much recent scholarship, given as it is to textual emendation and to solving problems of exegesis and interpretation by source criticism, has badly neglected this feature.

It will help to understand this characteristic of Biblical prediction to observe a clear case of it in the New Testament. Our Lord's great predictive discourse, known as the Olivet discourse, recorded in Luke 21, Mark 13, and in Matthew 24 and 25 was given in answer to essentially two questions of the disciples: what would be the sign of the Lord's second coming and when would the predicted destruction of Jerusalem occur? That the disciples may have supposed the two to be really one event does not alter this. The Lord's answer does not distinguish the two. Rather, since destructive judgments are prominent, aspects of both events, much of the discourse appears to be equally applicable to both. Some portions of the address may be applied only to one or to the other.

A clear Old Testament case is the Emmanuel prophecy of Isaiah 7:1-9:7. Practically every commentator agrees that all of this section is part of one oracle. At 7:14 a prophecy is made of the birth of a baby boy. The immediate context following applies the prophecy to the birth of Isaiah's son, Maher-shalal-hash-baz. (The reader is challenged to read Isaiah 7:14 through 8:4 and 8:18 to see if this is not true.) Yet the section closes at 9:6, 7 with a prediction which, evangelically handled, applies to Messiah Himself and to Him alone. The prophecy of 7:14, speaking in context so clearly of the birth of Isaiah's son as a sign to Ahaz and yet as we know from Matthew 1:23 speaking also of Messiah, is a case of this comprehensive grasp of the future wherein more than one even is involved in a single prediction.

The Babylon prophecy of Isaiah 13 and 14 abounds with this peculiar feature. Indeed, this is especially, though certainly not exclusively, an Isaiah characteristic.

Before proceeding let me succinctly state this principle. In presenting their messages, the prophets, without presenting a key to distinctions, frequently associated in one oracle items which though similar in some important particular are widely separated in time, and which may also be greatly different in other particulars. The prophets were essentially "seers" — men who saw truth in visual form as God granted them revelatory visions, and who wrote or told what they saw. Just as the dimension of depth cannot be incorporated into a two-dimensional picture except by illusion, so the element of depth (precise temporal relation) is often left out of the visions. Occasionally, as in the case of Jeremiah's prediction of the seventy years of captivity (Jeremiah 25) or Daniel's prediction of the seventy weeks (Daniel 7), this dimension is specially supplied. The fact remains that usually it was not. As will be seen shortly, this has an important bearing on a proper solution to the prophecies of the servant of the Lord in Isaiah.

A second important fact to be noted is that the entire book of Isaiah is a significant contribution to the development of the "promise doctrine" of the Old Testament. The promise to Abraham: "in thee shall all the families be blessed" (Genesis 12:3) supplies the very foundation for the existence of Israel as the special people of God — namely, in the process of time through Israel the whole world would be saved from the loss incurred by the fall of man. I have in my library a book containing the L. P. Stone lectures at Princeton Theological Seminary for 1902 - 1903. This work of 427 pages by Willis Judson Beecher is devoted to a thorough analysis of the Bible in relation to the promise to Abraham and is hence appropriately entitled, "The Prophets and the Promise." Beecher demonstrates that the servant prophecies of Isaiah 40-53 are a part of a connected development and shows that it is quite natural that the servant idea should contain both the nation and the personal Messiah who would come out of that nation. He also demonstrates that the connection of the servant with the promise to Abraham concerning his "seed" is certain, and that that seed is the personal Messiah. A similar connection with the Davidic covenant (II Samuel 7) is demonstrated. Beecher's pages cannot be summarized here; I must be satisfied to report his conclusions and to refer the interested reader to his work.

I have written of the comprehensive grasp of the future in Old Testament prediction and of the relation of Israel's prophecies to the Abrahamic promise as being significantly connected with the interpretation of the "servant." A third fact remains to be noted before spelling out my own statement of the Christian Messianic Interpretation. It is that the New Testament clearly teaches (here read carefully I Peter 1:1-12) that some Old Testament prophets, Isaiah in particular, made predictions of the future that neither they themselves nor their contemporaries were expected by God to understand — prophecies that were to be unravelled only after the coming of Christ and the effusion of the Spirit. Peter clearly states that these prophets who wrote by the power of the Holy Spirit of Christ searched their own writings to learn "what *time* or what manner of time the Spirit of Christ which was in them did point unto, when it testified beforehand the sufferings of Christ, and the glories that should follow them." Then he goes on to say that these prophecies of "the suffering and the glory" were not intended for the age of the prophets to understand but for the age of the New Testament church to understand (see I Peter 1:12).

This fact flies squarely in the face of the entire higher critical rejection of the possibility of true predictive prophecy. It likewise directly contradicts the higher critical contention that all prophecy is controlled by the historical background (*Sitz im Leben*) of the Prophecy. According to this latter notion, the prophet's message is restricted to the issues and problems of his own age, any reference to the remote future being typological or ideological only. The prophet might utter timeless truths, that is, applicable in many ages, but he could not foresee or predict an age in the future essentially different from his own. That Dr. North sees this issue is evident when he writes near the end of his book: "The fundamental objection to the traditional Messianic interpretation is that it is wedded to a too mechanical doctrine of inspiration. This seems to put it out of court as unworthy of serious consideration. The prophet is a mere amanuensis, and what he writes has no relevance to the circumstances of his own time. Morever, if this implies that he 'sees' in advance One who was not to come for another five or six centuries, it raises the difficult philosophical problem whether there can be an actual prevision of history" (*op. cit.* p. 207). It is interesting to observe that as a Christian (a most inconsistent one, I think) he must find some reference to Christ in the prophecies, but he does it on the basis of a kind of Platonic parable rather than of true prediction.

Christians may sometimes make great concessions to unbelief and still retain their faith in Jesus Christ as the very Son of God, but the Bible itself never makes such concessions. And let us all remember that there is not any evidence at all that Jesus ever subscribed to the "*Sitz im Leben*" (historical setting) limitations on Biblical interpretation. Quite to the contrary, it was He who said, "All things must be fulfilled, which are written in the law of Moses, and the prophets, and the psalms, concerning me" (Luke 24:44). There is an issue involved here too important to be ignored, too crucial to brush lightly over. It is the issue of faith versus unbelief, of deism versus supernaturalism, of Christianity versus anti-Christianity. If God be God then let him be God; if not, then let Baal be God! If God is the omniscient, omnipotent, omnipresent personal being the Bible and Christianity say He is, then He can know the future, He can determine the future. He can tell His prophets about it, and they can write it down for future generations to read. This is the persistent claim of Isaiah's God in the latter half of Isaiah. Says He: "I am Jehovah, that is my name; and my glory will I not give to another, neither my praise unto graven images. Behold, the former things are come to pass, and new things do I declare; before they spring forth I tell you of them" (Isaiah 42:8, 9). The entire forty-first chapter is devoted to this proof of God's existence — that is, that He is able to predict the future.

It is certain that prophecies usually can be related to some historical situation. Revelation is given *into* culture and does not originate in it. Context sometimes (eg. the virgin and her child, Isaiah 7:14) supplies the main data of the historical setting. As historical, linguistic, and archaeological studies enlarge knowledge of the historical setting of a prophecy, understanding of it is frequently enhanced. But the fact remains that extensive knowledge of the historical setting is often not supplied in context and is frequently incapable of recovery. Yet those prophecies were written "for our admonition." Furthermore, in the case of true prediction of the remote future, the age of the prophet cannot, in the very nature of the case, "control" the prophecy. Furnish the categories, terms, symbols, etc. it must. Language itself belongs to some period and changes with the passage of time. Any language is likewise obviously best qualified to express the ideas of the age in which it is in common use. But to say that God cannot bring foreign ideas before the eyes of a prophet's mind, ideas of which without a miracle he would never have thought, is to deny God's power. It cannot be done, of course, in a vacuum. It must be in terms of the prophet's own mind and culture. But its content can be totally foreign to both the mind of the prophet and his culture. That is to say, the events predicted may have no direct application at all to the prophet's age.

It should be clear, whether we like it or not, that to reject the possibility that predictive prophecy can take place is to reject Christianity. It should be equally clear that the fulfillment of predictive prophecy is one of the strongest divine testimonies to the truth of Christianity.

This excursion into the necessity for and importance of predictive prophecy to a Christian interpretation has interrupted exposition of the Christian Messianic interpretation. The topic may now be resumed.

The servant of the Lord in Isaiah 40-53 is several times specifically declared to be the nation Israel. About this no doubt can be entertained. At least once he is the "messengers" of the Lord, evidently referring to the prophetic order. This is at 44:26, which reads, "that confirmeth the word of his servant, and performeth the counsel of his messengers." It is possible that the first clause should be translated, "that confirmeth the word *about* his servant" in a manner parallel with the second clause. This would empty the passage of any identification of the servant with the prophetic order. Inasmuch, however, as the usual translation makes good sense and is capable of adjustment with the whole context, it probably should be retained. In 42:18-20 the servant is a somewhat unsuccessful messenger. The servant is also a saviour—both of Israel and of the Gentiles (49:5, 6). Finally, he is a patient sufferer who suffers (50:4-9) and dies (Isaiah 53) for the sins of "many" or "all."

There is a natural interpretation of all these facts which incorporates all into one synthetic view—the Christian Messianic Interpretation. Christ as the promised "seed of Abraham" is the one through whom Israel as God's servant blesses the world. As the consummation of the line of prophets, God's final messenger (Hebrews 1:1, 2), he executes the requirements of the servant as a prophet. As Son of God He obediently becomes the Lamb who "taketh away the sin of the world," thus carrying out the predictions of the servant's suffering and substitutionary death. The nation Israel as a messianic nation, their spiritual "elite" as the special bearers of the messianic consciousness of the nation, their prophets as the special witnesses of the messianic prospects, their kings and priests as administrators in their respective realms of the day-to-day functions of the messianic people —all have their consummation in Christ. This is what is meant in the traditional expositions of Jesus' work as "prophet, priest, and king."

Different scholars have described this concept in different ways while agreeing on the idea itself. Delitzsch has said it well: "The idea of 'the servant of Jehovah' assumed, to speak figuratively, the form of a pyramid. The base was Israel as a whole; the central section was that Israel, which was not merely Israel according to the flesh but according to the spirit also; the apex is the person of the Mediator of salvation springing out of Israel. And the last of the three is regarded (1) as the centre of the circle of the promised kingdom—the *second* David; (2) the centre of the circle of the people of salvation — the *second* Israel; (3) the centre of the circle of the human race — the *second* Adam. Throughout the whole of these prophecies in ch. xl.-lxvi. the knowledge of salvation is still in its second stage, and about to pass into the third. Israel's true nature as a servant of God, which had its roots in the election and calling of Jehovah, and manifested itself in conduct and action in harmony with this calling, is all concentrated in Him, the One, its ripest fruit. The gracious purposes of God towards the whole human race, which were manifested even in the election of Israel, are all brought by Him to their full completion" (*Commentary on Isaiah,* vol. II., pp. 174, 175).

Alexander suggests the figure of a body (Israel) and its head (Messiah) as an illustration of the organic connection of the elements of the servant prophecies (*Isaiah Translated and Explained,* vol. II, pp. 101-106, 279-282), but the interpretation is essentially the same. There have been others who use the figure of concentric circles. What the figure used for illustration may be is not important. The idea is the important thing.

The practice of referring to a group or nation as if they were a single person was more perfectly natural in ancient Israel and among her neighbors than it is for us. (It is not so uncommon now as might be supposed. In fact, it has already happened in this paragraph.) The ancient Hebrews frequently applied personal names to nations and tribes. Examples are Ashur (Assyria), Mitzraim (Egypt), and Israel (the Hebrews), as well as all twelve tribes of Israel (Simeon, Benjamin, Levi, Ephraim, etc.). This is carried out so thoroughly that frequently only the context and inflection of a proper name will tell, in the case of names of founders of nations especially, if the founder, himself, the country which bears his name, or the persons who compose it are meant. If the word is used with masculine plural verbal inflections agreeing, then the people of the country are meant. If the agreeing words are feminine singular, then the country is meant. If they are masculine singular, then either the country or its founder is probably meant. This is not to say that the Hebrews did not think of making distinctions between the tribe or nation and its founder, or between the nation and various individual members (as extreme statements of these features occasionally seem to imply).

It follows, therefore, that the comprehensive, Christian, Messianic interpretation of evangelical scholarship is the natural interpretation of Isaiah's prophecies of the Lord's servant.

Christians may rejoice that the most extensive studies of this subject published in recent generations, recognized even by rationalistic critics as superb scholarly productions, have been made by Christian advocates of a Christian Messianic Interpretation.

This chapter cannot present all the rational arguments and evidence confirming the Messianic view. Neither is this the place to present at length further reasons for rejecting other views. Even if this could be done it would not produce final results. One cannot prove Christianity true aside from the divinely accredited messengers of the New Testament (Jesus and the apostles) and of the Old Testament (Moses and the prophets). Inductive procedures, however objective and well conducted, do not produce certainty in the social and physical sciences and cannot do so in matters of religion and faith. Men have not often become Christians because of inductively established convictions but because of the testimony of messengers who for some reason or other they felt were trustworthy. Likewise Christian faith rests for its object not upon propositions proved true by science but upon revelation delivered by God Almighty—and of course upon Christ Himself.

Nevertheless, when the Old Testament predictions of Christ are seen in relation to His career, Christian faith is strengthened immeasurably. This is true today just as it was in apostolic times. Likewise the same thing will, when the Spirit of God illuminates the heart, frequently bring unbelievers to conviction and to faith.

Therefore, we cannot say to the reader, Read these pages of exposition of Isaiah and if convinced become a Christian. No, God "now commandeth all men every where to repent: Because he hath appointed a day, in the which he will judge the world in righteousness by that man whom he hath ordained (Jesus Christ); whereof he hath given assurance unto all men, in that he hath raised him from the dead" (Acts 17:30, 31). Since Jesus arose from the dead, there is not one good reason for continuing in disbelief. But we can say, Read and see if the Scriptures do not likewise show these things to be true.